THE 27 UNBREAKABLE RULES

BUILD A $100M+ BRICK + MORTAR CPG BRAND

DR. MARK YOUNG

FOREWORD BY DR. BENJAMIN HARDY

ISBN: [978-1-968339-91-3] (ebook)

ISBN: [978-1-968339-92-0] (paperback)

ISBN: [978-1-968339-93-7] (hardcover)

For more information about Mark Young and *The 27 Unbreakable Rules*, scan the QR code below:

ADVANCE PRAISE

For *The 27 Unbreakable Rules* and Mark Young

"Mark Young thinks differently, works harder and cares more than almost anyone I know in business. He's spent decades turning ideas into thriving CPG brands, and this book is the closest you'll get to having him as a mentor. Read it and you'll understand why so many people trust him."

—Joe Polish, *Wall Street Journal* bestselling author of *What's in It for Them* and founder of Genius Network

"With decades of advertising experience and a deep knowledge of the expectations of brick-and-mortar retailers, Dr. Mark Young knows what it takes to build a successful brand. Whether looking to scale their business or just starting out, *The 27 Unbreakable Rules* provides clear, specific knowledge that allows the reader to assess their readiness for the next step. This is a must read for anyone looking to increase their retail sales."

—Gino Wickman, author of *Traction and Shine*, creator of EOS

"Mark Young understands something that's becoming rare in today's abstract, digital marketplace—how to create and grow real products that people see, touch, buy and love to keep buying. In one of the most competitive industries anywhere, he is consistently creating a pioneering company and process that has no competition. *The 27 Unbreakable Rules* lays out exactly how he does it and how you can also grow your products and marketplace—with Mark's help."

—Dan Sullivan, cofounder of Strategic Coach®

To every inventor, dreamer, tinkerer and visionary who ever abandoned all common sense and fearlessly marched into the labyrinth known as consumer-packaged goods.

CONTENTS

FOREWORD

BY DR. BENJAMIN HARDY

One of my favorite quotes comes from the billionaire James Dyson, who created Dyson Vacuums. He said, "People don't want all-purpose. They want high-tech specificity."

This is one of the many places people go wrong with building companies, products and even in their marketing.

Most people attempt to be all-purpose, or broader and more generalist than they should be. They pack in several different components or solutions to try capturing a broader segment of the market. Then, in their marketing, they attempt "being everywhere" rather than crushing it in the right distribution channel.

Peter Thiel, a founder of PayPal with Elon Musk as well as a cofounder of Palantir, talks about the importance of applying "the power law" to distribution. What he means is that, if you get one distribution channel right, you can build an amazing company.

The problem people have in business, again, is that just like building their products and services and attempting to be too "all-purpose," they attempt too many distribution channels.

They never master one. They never focus on the distribution channel that actually produces the results.

I learned this lesson when I was a PhD student at Clemson University and wanted to become a professional author. Specifically, I wanted to get a six-figure book deal with a major New York publisher before completing my PhD. However, I discovered that less than 1 in 10,000 aspiring writers will ever get such a deal. Maybe even closer to 1 in 100,000.

Because my goal was so high and outlierish, and because I gave myself only a few years rather than a decade, I needed to find the most direct and powerful pathway to my goal. I needed an efficient way to get hundreds of thousands of email subscribers to prove to the big publishers that I could help them sell books and that I was serious.

If my goal had been lower, I could have utilized many different "pathways" to grow my "brand" or audience. But because my goal was so high, most pathways wouldn't work. Therefore, I had to find a hyper-efficient and focused path and truly go all in on that, leaving the other pathways behind.

It only took 18 months from when I committed to that goal to get a $220,000 book deal with a Big Five publisher for what became *Willpower Doesn't Work*, my first major book. I got there by focusing on one channel—which back then was blogging on Medium.com and driving blog traffic to an opt-in page where I gathered emails. I didn't attempt to blog on Medium, build a Twitter *and* do YouTube videos.

I didn't try everything. I focused on one distribution path that could get me to my singular objective.

I'm not telling you this from a tactical perspective. I'm not telling you that you should have my goal, or that you should deploy my pathway. Tactics change all the time. Medium.com doesn't even really exist anymore. I myself would never use Medium today.

That's not the point.

The point, which Mark Young is a unique master of, is for you to get truly strategic and specific. Stop being too broad in the products you make and the distribution paths you attempt.

Stop being a novice and amateur.

Raise your floor, get focused and commit to the power law —which are the few inputs that create almost all of the outputs.

There are few people I know that are as good, truly good, as Mark Young. He's an incredible husband and father, a man of faith who loves God, and he loves people. He loves his clients and wants them to succeed.

He's one of the few masters out there, in a world of generalists attempting to be everything to everyone. He is a master marketer that truly knows how to help people build the right product offerings, get those into retail stores and then blow them up through mass media.

He is a master.

I can say with absolute confidence and conviction that Mark understands deeply what he's doing.

This book will transform your life and business. It will transform and elevate how you think about what you're building and how you market that.

If you apply what you learn in this book, you can scale what you're doing. You'll understand the principles required to create a scalable product, then get it into a scalable distribution channel—which most miss.

If you apply what you learn in this book, you will escape the noise of 99 percent of the "competition" out there, "competition" that has broad and mediocre products and that attempts the common distribution channels which fail to deliver.

Mark will help you escape the noise and became a rare signal in the market. If you have enough conviction, Mark will challenge you to go big rather than stay small. He'll challenge you to get your product into Walmart and some of the other biggest retail stores in the world. He'll challenge you to shift from selling hundreds of units monthly to tens of thousands, and doing something powerful and significant.

You can trust this man. I wrote about him in my book, *The Science of Scaling*, for a reason. He's the real deal. But more importantly, I've had him in my home. He's been a blessing to my family. Both of us share the unique connection of having adopted a girl from Guatemala.

I consider Mark one of the few people I truly look up to. I love his mastery, his integrity, his faith.

Read this book deeply and go big. No more playing small. No more being an amateur.

—Dr. Benjamin Hardy, cofounder of Scaling.com and author of *The Science of Scaling*®, *10x Is Easier Than 2x*® and *Who Not How*®

PREFACE

If you are reading this book, I want to start by saying thank you, and in the immortal words of my spiritual adviser and life coach Ozzy Osbourne, "Aaaaaalll aboard!! Hahaha!" You are stepping onto the "Crazy Train," because if you are reading this book, you are like me; you are a visionary, an entrepreneur, a challenger who is driven by passion and purpose. Addicted to more, there is always a better way, and when others see problems you see opportunities. You created when others gave up. You heard phrases like "No," "That's impossible" and "You're crazy" so often they almost felt like nicknames. And you see every day as a new opportunity to create something where nothing exists, to create exponential value and make the world a better place. The best part of all—your life journey, just like mine, has brought you to the crazy world of consumer-packaged goods.

Why Should You Listen to Me?

There is an old saying: "An expert is someone that knows one more thing than you do." In reality, if I only knew one thing more than you, I might not be all that helpful to you. But when it comes to launching new products into retail, there are very few people that have my experience.

My name is Mark Young and I am a PhD. However, the doctor's connotation is not why you should pay attention to me. If you are about to launch (or are in the process of launching) a new product to consumers, wouldn't it make sense to follow the advice of those that have already successfully done what you are doing?

Over the past 30 years, I have helped entrepreneurs such as yourself launch hundreds of new products successfully. My work has amounted to sales that are measured in the billions of dollars. There is hardly any major retailer in the country that does not contain products on shelf that are represented by my firm or that got there because of our efforts.

Many of these companies have grown to become category leaders, while many others have been sold for astounding numbers. Recently, one of our clients, a simple grooming product launched only a few years prior, sold for 325 million dollars in cash.

In addition to helping hundreds of brands build their business, I have also launched my own brands. I personally know what it feels like to mortgage your home, borrow against your 401K and bet your entire future on your belief in yourself and your product.

I know what the butterflies in your stomach feel like when you have to financially commit to an advertising campaign, decide on a manufacturer or must find enough money to get your product manufactured.

Although our track record should impress anyone entering this field, there is another element that is perhaps even more important. That is that I have already made or witnessed every wrong way to launch a product and every mistake that young companies make. In other words, what I can save you from may well be what saves your business.

Allow me to give you another reason you can't go this alone by sharing an out-of-industry example. One of my passions, besides helping entrepreneurs grow their business, is racing cars. In fact, I hold a Guinness World Record in auto racing. I am now driving at pro level and am a nationally certified instructor.

When my fellow instructors or I take a first-time driver on the track, we do something called lead/follow. The students' job is to drive behind us and put their car in the same place on the track where we put ours. Now, many of these young drivers show up excited and ready to get on the track. They are often convinced that between all their experiences on the street and the fact that they have watched all nine *Fast & Furious* movies, they will be fast drivers and probably as fast or faster than we instructors.

The reality is, without exception, that these inexperienced racetrack drivers are white-knuckling and driving at their absolute maximum speed while we instructors are literally drinking coffee, talking on cell phones or radios and never at any time needing to apply our brakes. The gap is that significant. If the students were to attempt to do what an experienced race driver can do, they would absolutely crash, no question.

Why is this? It is simple—as experienced race drivers, we see things that the new driver can't hope to see. The reason is unconscious awareness. As instructors and racers, we have many, many hours on these tracks. And because we do long, multi-hour races, we have hundreds of laps of the track all recorded in our unconscious mind. We see things on the track, know where to turn in, know where to brake and know when to accelerate without even having to think about it.

There is a theory called the "10,000-Hour Rule." The idea is based on the work of Dr. Anders Ericsson and made popular by

Malcom Gladwell's 2008 book *Outliers*. The core of this theory is that it takes time and consistent, deliberate practice to master something. Natural talent helps, but on average it is around 10,000 hours to master a skill. Breaking this down—at 50 hours per week, mastery takes four to five years.

Now think of how many different skillsets you will need to successfully launch and build your brand: marketing, legal, accounting, distribution, manufacturing, financing, research and development. You would need a lifetime in this industry to accumulate that much knowledge and experience.

I have a lifetime of experience in the world of consumer-packaged goods (CPG) and even so, I still turn to other experts who know their domain better than me.

Chances are, if you are reading this book, you are that first-time driver entering the race called CPG marketing. You have not yet had the exposure to develop the skills of an experienced person in this industry, just like we as race car drivers all had to have our first day on the track. You cannot be expected to know or have the expertise of someone with decades of experience and hundreds of successful product launches. It is simply not realistic to go it alone.

The truth is, you are not being fair to yourself or your company if you expect to have all the answers right now.

What Are Your Odds?

Let's look at some stats. According to a Harvard Business School study, there are 30,000 new consumer products introduced to the country every year. 85% of these new products are developed by large, established brands. Of all the new products launched this year, 95% will fail. That means that only 1,500 new consumer products will make it this year—and out of that 1,500, 1,275 are from big existing brands. This means that you are competing to be one of only 225 successful new products.

That puts your odds for success at .0075%. While it is better odds than buying a lotto ticket, it is worse odds than placing your money on 17 at a roulette table.

Now the question for you to consider is, "What are my odds and those of my company?" In any given year, our success on a new product launch is 95% to 100% success. How is this possible? First, we do not work with clients that have bad products or bad business practices, so that improves our odds substantially. Next, we know how to prevent our clients from making deadly mistakes early in their history, preventing them from melting down before they ever launch.

Because we are so focused on client success, we also have a rule that we do not work with people that we cannot build a real relationship with or people that are incapable of learning new things.

The next thing is that we have created the system, or the algorithm, to launch new products. This is a tried-and-true pathway that every product must travel. With each step you miss, your odds of success go down; it is that simple. The goal of this book is to teach you these proven steps and to help you avoid deadly mistakes along the path.

Another reason to listen to me is because I have been where you are. I am not just another consultant. Honestly, my opinion of consultants is that they are like a guy who shows up to an orgy claiming to know 50 ways to have sex, but without a date.

I co-launched my first product when I was about 13 years old; it was called Kangaroo Shoes. It was essentially a small coil spring attached to a platform that you strapped onto your foot, similar to that of an old-timey roller skate. With these on your feet, you could hop around and jump fairly high. (This product would probably never get past the liability lawyers today.) I even marketed the product by dressing up in a kangaroo costume and bouncing around state fairs. I had zero idea what I was doing but did manage to get the product into the now-defunct Toys "R" Us chain.

Later, with much more time in the industry and with a different product, I borrowed all the equity from our home, borrowed against our 401K and wired all the money to a factory in China, to people I had never actually met in person.

Lucky for me (I believe we make most of our luck) that bet turned into a 10 million dollar instant hit and, as they say, the rest is history. I know firsthand what it feels like to bet everything on yourself, which is how the really great entrepreneurs do it.

Do You Have What It Takes?

The world of entrepreneurship is not for everyone. As my friend and creator of the EOS (Entrepreneurial Operating System) Gino Wickman says: "Entrepreneurs are not made; we are born this way." Gino points out that about four percent of the population is genetically predisposed to living the entrepreneurial lifestyle. In fact, entrepreneurs have made up about four percent of the population for the past 250 years or more.

What makes that lifestyle so different is that we live in a world with no guarantees, other than the guarantee that nothing will go as planned. We entrepreneurs have an extremely high tolerance for risk, and we are willing to push forward on a project or idea when everyone around us is telling us it can't be done. Should you want to find out if you are a natural entrepreneur, I suggest Gino's book, *Entrepreneurial Leap: Do You Have What It Takes to Become an Entrepreneur?* It is available on Amazon.

If you are launching a new product and business into the retail space, understand that the first 18 to 36 months are not about making a lot of money or, in some cases, not about making any money. This period of time is about proof of concept; it is about establishing yourself in the category and proving you and your product worthy of belonging in that category. This is a time that takes great discipline, self-sacrifice and emotional control. Remember the odds? Entrepreneurs are the rare group of people that can live day to day with uncertainty, not knowing if they will have money for payroll next month.

In Jordan Peterson's best-selling book *12 Rules for Life: An Antidote to Chaos*, his seventh rule is "Pursue what is meaningful, not what is expedient." He explains that society and success in general are built by those people willing to make short-term sacrifices for long-term benefits. Or as he says it another way, "If you give up something of value now, you can bargain with the future for something better."

As two dear friends of mine, Dan Sullivan, founder of Strategic Coach®, and Dr. Benjamin Hardy perfectly explain in their book *10X Is Easier Than 2X*®, most people live in fear or with a scarcity mindset. These people are focused on what they need, such as paying the rent, food, shelter, a car or maybe even a vacation. Their focus is on their needs. And with a scarcity mindset, they often feel that for them to earn a dollar, someone else must give up a dollar. In other words, it is a zero-sum game. The scarcity mindset says there is only so much wealth to pass around.

But real entrepreneurs live with an abundance mindset. We know that wealth can be created. It is not a fixed or finite number; we know that we can bring value to the world and that value creates more wealth.

An example would be Bill Gates. Regardless of what you think of him as a person, he is an incredibly wealthy person. Microsoft has made him tens of billions of dollars. But now let me ask you who really made the most money off Microsoft? It was not Bill Gates; it was all of us.

You see, the Microsoft operating system changed how

computers could function and who had access to all this computer power. Suddenly, the world had access to affordable computer power, increasing the efficiency of nearly every human in America and most of the world. It saved companies millions of man hours on otherwise mundane and long, drawn-out tasks. Bill Gates did not just earn a lot of money; he created wealth for the world, and in return, he got to keep a small portion of that wealth.

You get into being an entrepreneur not out of what you need or fear; you get into it based on what you want. As Dan explains in *10X Is Easier Than 2X*, "Needs have to be explained; wants do not. You simply want them."

Why the 27 Rules?

What would you do if you knew you could not fail? It's an interesting question, right?

The goal of this book is to create a guide that—if followed perfectly—would result in 100 percent success for the reader. The goal is literally a "Can't Fail" guide to the world of CPG. The 27 rules are simply absolute attributes that every successful CPG entrepreneur has lived by. The more of the 27 rules you adhere to, the better your chances of success. Follow them all and you can't miss.

Who Is This Book Written For?

This book should be a must-read for anyone involved in launching, manufacturing or marketing any consumer-packaged product—entrepreneurs, inventors, brand managers, private equity investors and anyone that has ever dreamt of launching their own product into retail. This is your rulebook.

PART I

PRODUCT

RULE 1

DON'T MAKE PRODUCTS YOU DON'T BELIEVE IN

"The moment you doubt whether you can fly, you cease forever to be able to do it."
—Peter Pan

There are many reasons for this rule, one of which is the ability and desire to take risks. If your company is a startup or in its early stages, there will come a time when you will need to go all in. Do not fall victim to other people's money stories. Getting investors is exceedingly difficult and sometimes impossible. As an investor myself, I am never going to invest in a business where the founder is not up to his or her eyeballs in the operation.

I am never going to put money into a business where the founder does not have his or her own money sunk into the business. I want to know that the founders feel so strongly about their business that they are willing to risk it all to succeed. I want to know that the entrepreneur does not have a plan B, that they have metaphorically burned all the boats and that there is no way through for them except for success.

Something you can always count on is that it is not *"Will*

there be tough times?" it is "*When* will there be tough times?" You will need to be all in. It is impossible to be all in on a product you do not truly believe in.

Another reason that you should not make a product you do not believe in is authenticity. In your early days, you will be the chief salesperson for your company. No matter if you are raising capital, selling your product at a trade show or meeting with a buyer at Walmart, your authentic feelings and belief in the product will come through. No one is signing on with you when you are not believable.

Allow me to give you an early all-in story from my past. One of my dearest friends was the game show legend Chuck Woolery. Now, as close as we were, we did not share a passion for fishing. Chuck would fish every day, morning to night, if he had the time to do it, while I thought fishing was like watching paint dry.

One day I got a call from Chuck saying he had just met a man that makes a motorized fishing lure, and that this man was going to give up because he couldn't get it off the ground. Chuck told me that we needed to buy the company.

This was a time in my life when my career was just getting some traction so the idea of spending my money on fishing was not appealing. To complicate this issue, Chuck was in the middle of a nasty and costly divorce and could not make any investments.

Chuck proceeded to say he was sending me some of the product and told me, "Just look at it and you will get it." A few days later, I received some poorly packaged fishing lures. The lure had a string that came out of the mouth of what looked like a little minnow. When you connected your fishing line to the string and cast it out, the string pulled out like a kid's pull toy and the little lure "swam" and fluttered about on the surface of the water like an injured minnow.

I did not need to be a fisherman to understand that this

worked, and not only would it hook fish, it would also hook fishermen. Chuck and I made a deal to buy the majority of this fledgling company and it was my job to figure out how to sell it.

At the time, QVC was a major retailer of novel new items, so I presented the product to them. Their opinion was that it was cool and unique, but QVC had a bad history of selling products for men. However, because they knew me and because I had Chuck Woolery as an on-air guest, they said they would give it a shot.

Now, what you need to keep in mind is that when you sell product to QVC, it is basically a consignment deal until you have really established yourself as a success. So if the product did not sell, I would get it back, with no plan B on what to do with this inventory.

I had to decide how much I believed in this item. The truth is that I was all in on this product, but I was really all in on Chuck Woolery's ability to connect with the female audience that watched QVC. I believed that even though products for men had failed at QVC, he would not, since women would fall in love with him, believe him and buy it. Just as important, I believed in my buddy Chuck. I knew he was in love with this product and that his authenticity would shine through to TV viewers.

What happened next was that "dark night of the soul." I had to decide just how all in I really was. It was one thing to believe in the product and Chuck, but to pull this off, I was going to have to mortgage our home, borrow all of our cash and our retirement savings and send all our money to a factory in China, to people I had never met in person. Then I had to believe that we could sell it on a TV network known for failing with men's products. This was a real "put your money where your mouth is" moment.

I took the entrepreneur's leap. I borrowed everything and had the product manufactured and sent to QVC. Now, just in case I might have been getting a glimmer of confidence, QVC decided to give us an eight-minute airing at 7 pm on a Tuesday night that just happened to be election day. It would have been difficult to get a worse time slot.

But Chuck went on air with the confidence and excitement that can only happen when someone is 100 percent in. He told the TV audience how much he loved the lure, how he used it every day and how he even outperformed pro fisherman with it. This was all so true and so heartfelt that the audience knew he was telling the truth.

What happened next is one of those days that gets locked in your memory. In those eight minutes, Chuck sold out the entire inventory and had the product going on a wait list. He made the product that we named MotoLure the biggest product of the day and set records for the most successful male product ever on QVC.

Right after leaving the set and going back into the green room, we were joined by the buyer and the QVC Vice President, who asked me if I was available to meet with them the following morning. I told her I had a 7:30 am flight back home. She then asked, "Are you available in the morning if I give you a purchase order for several million dollars for more Moto-Lures?" to which I responded, "What time is good for you?"

Chuck and I went on to sell this item by the millions, and it expanded into Chuck Woolery sunglasses, vests, hats, fishing rods, auto accessories and even personal care products. We were now a fourth-quarter regular guest and doing numbers in excess of $40,000 per minute, which is probably $70,000 per minute in today's dollars.

The point is that had I not believed in the product and my partner, I never would have taken this risk. Had I not believed in the product and my TV talent, I never would have convinced QVC to take a risk on a male product. Finally, had Chuck

Woolery not truly had the passion for this little fishing lure, the TV audience would never have bought it.

To summarize: Don't make products you don't believe in—because if you don't, no one else will either.

Rule 1 Questions

- How strongly do you believe in your product?
- Are you willing to bet everything you have on it?
- Is it a product that you would personally use or recommend to your closest friends and relatives?

RULE 2

MAKE PRODUCTS THAT SOLVE PEOPLE'S PROBLEMS OR NEEDS

"It is not enough to be industrious; so are the ants. What are you industrious about?"
—Henry David Thoreau

Consumers do not buy products; they buy outcomes. You don't want cough medicine; you want to stop coughing. You do not have a Tylenol deficiency; you want to end a headache.

Often, an inventor will bring a product to us that has great technology because some engineers or the inventor themselves figured out how to do something, but the product does not actually solve a need.

Let me give you some examples. First, there's Juicero, a Silicon Valley high-tech startup that made and sold a high-end juicer, at $400 to $700. Customers would have to buy the over-engineered machine, have a monthly subscription and buy the single-serving juice packs. You would place the juice pack into the machine, and it would squeeze all the juice out for you.

Sounds amazing, doesn't it? Until people realized you could squeeze just as much juice out of the packs with your hands.

The company went out of business, taking millions in startup capital with it.

Another famous useless product was Google Glass. Obviously created by one of the most successful companies in existence, Google Glass was a pair of designer glasses that gave you a tiny computer screen on your face. Except it was hard to see, it didn't connect well and no one found a real reason to have a tiny screen on their face. Needless to say, even with the power of Google, it failed miserably.

Sometimes you can even make a useless product and sell it for a while until the public figures it out. Take the product Ab Roller. This was a device that was used while sitting on the floor to do sit-ups. The product did amazingly well for a while until the crew at *60 Minutes* did a segment on it and had experts discuss how it was no more useful for doing sit-ups than putting your feet under your bed. In just one day, the product was dead.

Finally, our last and most spectacular example: Segway. Introduced in 2001, it was considered a breakthrough in technology, a two-wheeled device that could balance itself and a rider. John Doerr, famed venture capitalist and the 40th richest man in the world, claimed it would be more important than the internet. Steve Jobs claimed it would surpass the personal computer. The comedy television show *South Park* dedicated an entire episode to it. However, sales did not meet expectations and as of now, the original product no longer exists and is out of production.

Because while everyone was amazed at the technology and its ability to balance, no one ever asked consumers if they needed a one-person vehicle that held no additional items, that only went 15 miles per hour, had a 15-mile range, took 12 hours to recharge and cost $5,000. (By the way, I successfully identified it as a loser the day it hit the market.) In other words,

Segway invented a $5,000 solution to a $300 problem—called an electric scooter.

The title of my dear friend Joe Polish's book, *What's in It for Them?* says it all; your product is not about your technology or how clever you are, it is about what is in it for the consumer. Every winning product meets a need.

Coca-Cola meets the need of thirst. A bottle of wine meets the need to be a great gift, a relaxing romantic evening or being able to unwind. The more defined the need, the better the possible success. So consider what need your product fulfills. Also keep in mind that products in the same category often fulfill different needs.

For example, a $25 handbag from Target fills the need to carry incidentals, such as a wallet or cell phone, in one spot. It may even fill the need to match a particular outfit that a woman is wearing.

Now, what need does a $3,500 Gucci handbag meet? It too will hold belongings and may match an outfit, but that is not why it was purchased. If it was purchased by a woman for herself, her deliverables include beauty, prestige, a sense of belonging to an exclusive group, pride of ownership and perhaps the tactile feel of the bag.

But what if it was purchased by her husband? What was his deliverable? For him, it may be that he knew she wanted it and providing his wife with the things she wants is its value to him. It could be he wanted to express to her that he will spend $3,500 frivolously on her because of his love for her. It may be that he wants other men to see how his wife is so cared for and pampered that she is out of their league. It could be they just had a bad fight and he wants to buy his way out of the doghouse.

The bottom line is that every product must meet the needs of people. It is your job to intimately understand those needs at a deep level and to figure out how you can best meet them.

Rule 2 Questions

- What need(s) does your product solve?
- What are the hidden, underlying reasons for consumers to buy it?
- Did you make the product because you could, or because it was a consumer need?

RULE 3

NEVER TRY TO BE EVERYTHING TO EVERYONE

"You can please some of the people all of the time, all of the people some of the time, but you can't please all of the people all of the time."
—Abraham Lincoln

Very few products appeal to everyone. Oftentimes, a new inventor or entrepreneur will contact us with a new item, and when we ask them who and what the demographic is they want to reach, they will say "everyone." The conversation will generally go like this: They will tell us they have invested in a new line of skin-care products they want to sell. We will say, "Great. Who does it appeal to?" and the caller will confidently say, "Anyone with skin." But this is not how the world of products works.

Let's use a car for example. A car is the thing for personal transportation; you go to work, shopping or on vacation. A car will allow you nearly unlimited freedom to travel. So why do some people buy a Prius, while others buy a pickup or a giant SUV? All of these choices move you from one place to another, and because of traffic and speed restrictions, they all do it at about the same pace.

But the Prius will do it more cost-effectively, so shouldn't it be the overall choice? If the only criteria were moving me from point A to point B for the least cost, it would be a top choice. But this is not how humans buy things.

I may buy the Prius as a political statement—to show that I care about the environment—while the pickup may be handy for work to haul things. But in reality, only 15% of pickup trucks are used for work. In fact, a recent *Axios* study found that 87% of pickups are used for commuting, shopping and errands. Most people buy a pickup because they like the look, the way it sits, the size and the versatility, but also what it says about them as a person. The same is true of the SUV.

Now, let's drill down even deeper. Let's look at Ferrari, Lamborghini and McLaren. All these cars fall into the supercar class of automobiles and have comparable price tags ranging from $300,000 on the low end to upwards of four million towards the top. They are all super high performance, with cutting-edge technology. You would think that these three brands compete with each other, but you would be wrong. All three brands have vastly different buyers:

Ferrari Buyers. These buyers usually join the Ferrari club within the first 30 days of ownership, and up to 85% of these cars are red. The brand message is sleek and refined racing technology combined with Italian luxury and style.

Lamborghini Buyers. These buyers are younger as a group and are most likely to live in a downtown condominium or apartment. The brand message is aggressive and exotic with sharp lines, wild colors and "in your face" styling.

McLaren Buyers. These buyers are minimalists and seek functionality. They are most likely to take the car to a racetrack or be a fan of Formula 1 (F1) racing. The brand message is clean, aerodynamic and built purely for performance.

These brands have different images and cultures attached to them:

Ferrari is the gentleman racer, seen as the most prestigious of the three brands and belonging to an exclusive club.

Lamborghini is the wild extrovert, associated with flashy lifestyles and bold personalities.

McLaren is the tech purist, appealing to the engineer, racer or F1 fan who is all about the performance.

The fact is, most Ferrari buyers do not visit a Lamborghini or McLaren dealership and vice versa. They do not really compete with each other. As a personal owner and fan of one of these three brands, I can tell you firsthand that I have rarely ever been in the dealership of the other two, and never with the intent to buy one.

Let's look at a category that you would think appeals to everyone: toothbrushes. You would assume that everyone buys toothbrushes, but you would be wrong. Ninety-two percent of the population brushes their teeth, meaning 8% have no use for the product. In fact, 23% of Americans go two or more days without brushing their teeth.

Think of the variations in toothbrushes: Waterpik, Sonicare, Oral-B, Colgate and more. Plus there are options within brands: hard, soft, massaging, cross action, deep reach, charcoal, kids and more. The list goes on and on.

We know that 92% of America buys a toothbrush. But not all of them want a battery-powered toothbrush, and of those people that do, not all of them want a high-end Waterpik toothbrush. So even a market as widespread as toothbrushes is not universal in appeal.

Nike made a fortune being the innovative leader in athletic shoes, collaborating with big sports stars like Michael Jordan. But today we see a quite different Nike; we see a company that is in a sales decline and financial difficulty. How did this happen? You may think it ramped up when Nike decided to step into the world of politics and support Colin Kaepernick and his kneeling during the national anthem. But this alone did not ruin the brand—in fact, the financial impact was posi-tive, even as some consumers began to boycott Nike.

At the same time, they decided to become a lifestyle brand, making golf clubs, clothing, tech devices and about any other category you can think of. They decided to launch their own stores, becoming competition to the retailers that helped make them.

Meanwhile, upstart brands like Hoka, Brooks and even Adidas put all their focus on innovating new shoes and conse-quently captured a large swath of Nike's market share. By the time the management at Nike figured out the problem, they were miles behind in shoe design and are struggling now to get back into the shoe innovation business, which is what the world wanted from them all along.

Even when we look at retailers, we see the same problem. Everyone knew of Kmart; they were around for decades and were famous for their "Blue Light Specials." Most people do not realize that the product mix at Kmart was nearly identical to the product mix at Target. It was almost the same store. So why did one prosper while the other one failed?

Target created the category of "Cheap Chic." They put their focus on in-store designer brands and trendy housewares, while Kmart stuck to the model of being everything to every-one. The result was that Kmart became a place that no one would even admit to shopping at, while people would brag about the deals and finds they got at Target. Kmart had brand recognition, but the brand was not desirable and meant nothing to anyone.

As Joe Polish often says, "The riches are in the niches." Given the choice of being a "me too" product to 340,000,000 Americans or being a must-have product for 5,000,000, take the five million.

When designing for a niche, you want to drill deep and solve a problem at a very emotional level. You want to speak your niche's language, using terms and names that resonate with that specific group. And you want to go beyond the utility and deliver on identity.

Here are a few examples of brands that found their "riches in the niches":

YETI

Niche: Hardcore outdoor enthusiasts, hunters and fishermen
Result: $1B-plus brand; now serves lifestyle and outdoor categories without losing its "rugged roots."

Dollar Shave Club

Niche: Men tired of overpriced razors
Result: Acquired by Unilever for $1B. Still a lean, male-focused grooming brand.

Warby Parker

Niche: Fashion-forward consumers desiring affordable designer eyewear
Result: $3B-plus valuation, expanded into physical retail and eye exams, but still niche-oriented.

Glossier

Niche: Millennials and Gen Z women wanting "skin-first," minimalist beauty
Result: Cult brand, $1B valuation, major retail expansion, but still not mainstream like L'Oréal or Estée Lauder.

RXBAR

Niche: Fitness-focused, label-conscious eaters (CrossFit & Paleo early adopters)
Result: Sold to Kellogg's for $600M. Expanded into kids and plant-based, but still in the "clean protein" space.

Chubbies Shorts

Niche: Millennial men wanting fun, retro, short shorts
Result: Built a cult following, then expanded into swim, casual-wear and more, but still niche-driven in tone.

GoPro

Niche: Extreme sports and action-video fans
Result: Went public; still dominant in its niche even as smartphone cameras improved.

Oatly

Niche: Vegan, lactose-intolerant and sustainability-conscious consumers
Result: IPO in 2021; grew oat milk from a niche to a mainstream shelf category.

Key Traits of Niche-Winning Brands

- **Hyper-specific positioning:** Solved a problem no one else focused on.

- **Simple, bold messaging:** Often started with one product and one promise.
- **Community-first marketing:** Many built loyal tribes before they built scale.
- **Strong DTC or online roots:** Let them test, grow and own their niche without retailer pressure.
- **Scaled without going generic:** Expanded smartly but stayed emotionally tied to their core user.

You don't need to serve everyone to win. In fact, unless you have a nearly limitless supply of cash, you will not be able to afford to share your message with everyone. These brands became household names because they focused on someone specific first and nailed the problem that group cared most about. Only then could they expand their universe of prospective consumers.

Rule 3 Questions

- Who is the real customer for your product?
- Are you appealing to a niche that is currently not served or is underserved?
- Can you describe your customer in detail, as if they are a friend?

RULE 4

NEVER BE A "ME TOO" PRODUCT

*"Always be a first-rate version of yourself, instead of a second-rate
version of somebody else."*
—Judy Garland

As of this writing, the nation has experienced some rapid inflation, which places pressure on every brand. Not only are brands competing within their own category of trade, but they are also competing with other items such as a tank of gas.

When studying the *IRI* and *Nielsen* reports (this is the actual scan data that shows what every brand sells at every major retailer), we see that the biggest growing brands in most categories fall into one of three classes. They are:

1. the store brand, which is the low price leader
2. the highest-priced product in the category, and
3. the brand with the largest advertising budget.

It is also not unusual to see the brand with the largest ad campaign also be the highest-priced item in the category.

Why this happens is quite simple. Consumers are not buying at the lowest price; they always buy the highest perceived value. Since they cannot afford to buy premium everything, they make decisions on what items are a commodity and what items are not. A commodity item is anything where the consumer sees every brand in the category as being equal or mostly similar to each other. What these items and categories are will vary between consumers.

Consumers are making a choice between the brands they cannot live without and the products they perceive as commodities. So the shopper may decide that they will save money and pick up store-brand green beans or corn since they see them as being equal in value, taste and outcomes, but then buy Heinz ketchup because they believe it is superior and better-tasting than the store brand. This is true in multiple categories, not just food items. It could be toilet paper, lotion, motor oil or underwear.

When anything is viewed as a commodity, then everything has the same perceived value, meaning the lowest price is the winner. A fitting example was the anti-itch category a few years back. At the time, the biggest advertiser and branded product in the category was Cortizone-10, a one percent hydrocortisone cream. However, all the generic store brands for anti-itch had the same one percent hydrocortisone in them. Consumers viewed these products as all being a commodity and consequently the store brand was the biggest seller in every chain.

To add to this story, we managed a client that rolled out an anti-itch product with new technology and without hydrocortisone. The product was safer and worked better, but it was higher priced. With the aggressive advertising campaign we developed for it, our client became the number one anti-itch product at retail in only weeks.

The reasons were simple: better technology, safer formula, faster results and a good, clear advertising message. With this new technology, suddenly a category that consumers had viewed as a commodity for years was no longer a commodity. There was now something different.

When developing your product, you have three options:

1. **Be the lowest-price provider,** which in nearly every case is a race to the bottom with no margins since someone in China will always beat you on price.

2. **Develop the best version of the product in the category.** You become the leader with the best ingredients, the best technology, the best packaging and, most importantly, with superior outcomes and performance for the consumer.

3. **Provide moderate- to high-quality products with a superior brand experience.** These are brands that make products that meet the cost of entry into a premium class. While they do not provide best-in-class tech, they provide a best-in-class customer experience.

What follows are some examples of superior brand experiences:

Old Spice. Objectively there are better-performing deodorants, but their brilliant branding created a unique and valuable brand experience. Old Spice took an old brand and made it hip and cool with "The Man Your Man Could Smell Like."

Method. Objectively not the most powerful cleaner, but the branding is hip, eco-friendly and includes design-centric packaging that elevates ordinary cleaners to lifestyle accessories. Method turned hand soap, a typical commodity item, into bathroom décor.

Beats by Dr. Dre. Objectively the quality is average for the premium price. In fact, most product reviews show just average audio quality. However, the branding and celebrity hip-hop lifestyle has turned it into a fashion accessory, giving it a "cool" factor and association that the consumer is happy to pay for.

Red Bull. Objectively this is not the best tasting or functional energy drink, but the brand elevates the customer experience through extreme sports and "Red Bull Gives You Wings" messaging. (Note: This has been altered to sometimes use "Red Bull Gives You Wiiings.") Red Bull's massive investment into F1, auto, motorcross, planes and boat racing has made it the drink of all things racing and extreme sports. They understand that people are passionate about their favorite sports and will support the brands that support the sport.

Starbucks. Objectively the coffee quality is lower than competitors and often has a burnt flavor to it. But when you look at the branding experience, they became people's third place. For many it became home, work and Starbucks. For its customers, Starbucks is about customization and status. People have ritualized their products—they want to be seen carrying a Starbucks coffee cup and will stand in line to get it.

Crocs. Objectively an ugly shoe that has unlimited alternatives. However the branding is fun, quirky, self-expressive and motivates people to buy them, literally as a cultural meme.

Ugg Boots. Objectively, like Crocs, they are not that great; they overheat, are not durable and have tons of competition. But looking at the branding, they are a lifestyle phenomenon. They are comfortable, California-cool and have tremendous celebrity adoption.

Jeep Wrangler. Objectively poorly designed, rough-riding, with mediocre reliability and poor fuel economy. Why buy it? The branding. It equals freedom, adventure and rugged Americana, and the owners feel part of a tribe. To drive a Jeep is to belong to a group of people that love adventure, even if the truck has never left the highway.

What do all these brands share? Emotional identity, community and belonging, cultural relevance, focus on packaging and presentation and consistency of messaging. They say the same thing over and over until it becomes a universal truth. You don't always have to build the best product if you can build the best story and emotional connection.

Rule 4 Questions

- If your product was not on the shelf, could I find an adequate alternative to it?
- If consumers see your product next to your competitor, can they clearly identify and understand why your item is superior and delivers better outcomes?
- Are there clear and real points of difference between your product and the competition?

RULE 5

MAKE PRODUCTS THAT FIT ONE OF THE THREE PATHWAYS TO RETAIL

"You won't win unless you learn how to lose."
—Kareem Abdul-Jabbar

Most new start-up items are launched in e-commerce and on Amazon, which has unlimited capabilities. The reason for this is that for Amazon to present it to the public, they merely need to add another digital product offering. Next, Amazon just needs to find some space for your item in a warehouse, and they are constantly upgrading and expanding their warehouse capabilities.

But brick-and-mortar retail is vastly different. Retail stores are limited by physics; retail is controlled by atoms. Which is a fun way of saying it is limited by the number of real, physical things you can put on a shelf that has finite space. After all, Walgreens can't just add a new metal building to the back of 8,000 stores to hold more product.

Every inch of shelf space in every retailer in America is accounted for; these product sets are known as planograms. Planograms are set once per year, every square inch is accounted for and the planogram is executed in the same fashion across the country. In fact, all the major retailers have a model store with no customers in it, just for the retail buyers physically working on and manipulating their planogram for the coming year. Those buyers are tasked with producing as much profit as possible for their assigned planogram.

In order for your product to go onto a retailer's shelf, some other product must come off to make space for yours. It is that simple. But if your new product does not yet have a winning sales record, it is an uphill battle, since the retail buyer already knows what the current product assortment sells for them versus your yet-to-be-determined sales velocity, which is how well your product sells off the shelf when it is available.

To assist the retail buyer with the design of the planogram, retailers have adopted a system known as SKU rationalization. Here is how this works: Assume we have a category with 20 different items in the plan, and the 20 items combined sell for 20 million dollars per year. SKU rationalization has the retail buyer analyzing the answer to this question: What would consumer behavior be if one of the 20 products were missing? Will the consumer walk away and go to a competing store to buy it? Or will they just transfer their buying decision to one of my remaining 19 items?

Let's use mouthwash as an example. Assume we have three flavors of the exact same brand of mouthwash: peppermint, spearmint and cinnamon. If the research shows that a cinnamon buyer would indeed buy spearmint in the absence of cinnamon, that product is likely cut from the shelf. This way, the retailer has a new "hole" on the shelf to fill. They have the opportunity to sell something more. It could be with another mouthwash, but that space could also be used for the category right next to the mouthwash. What and who gets to be the new item entering the retailer is determined by what product will make them the most money.

Because of these facts, there are really only three models you can follow to get your item or brand into the major retailers. For some products, it is possible to meet two of the three criteria, but without at least one, your odds of getting in are slim.

Model 1: Category Expander

This is exactly what it sounds like. It means your product has the ability to increase the actual size of a category. A great example of this would be fabric softener. Years ago, the only thing a shopper bought to clean their clothes was some brand of detergent. But then came the invention of fabric softener, which meant that a good homemaker would now walk out of the store with two items to do the laundry instead of just one. This category has seen many expansions, such as Wisk for a "ring around the collar" and OxiClean for brighter whites.

Another example of a category expander story is hair conditioner. Conditioners, or "rinses" as they were originally called, really started in the 1930s, but it was not until the '50s that they became a real product. The first big player in the category was Suave due the fact that they launched an aggressive TV campaign explaining to women why they needed a second bottle of product for their hair. In this case, the success was not won by the first company to make hair conditioner; it was the first company to advertise it. Haircare now has several category expanders, such as split end treatments, shampoo for dyed hair, blow dryer treatments, shine products and many more.

Any time you can show the retail buyer that consumers will walk out with more stuff, you have a shot (assuming all the other attributes have been met) as you are expanding the revenue from that buyer's planogram.

Model 2: Trade Up

"Trading up" is when you can demonstrate to a buyer that consumers who traditionally buy a product at a given price will opt for your higher-priced product as an alternative. Let's look at the math from the retail buyer's perspective. If my store runs at a 37% margin and you can get a consumer to trade up from a $5 item to an $8 item, my retailer just made 37% of the additional $3.

But you must keep in mind that this takes a lot more than just walking in with a higher-priced item. You must prove that you can sell your higher-priced product in sufficient volume to warrant the shelf space.

An example would be Ragú pasta sauce versus Botticelli pasta sauce. A bottle of Ragú Old World Style Traditional sauce sells for $1.79 as of this writing. A bottle of Botticelli sells for $4.99, which is more than double. We have been very successful in getting consumers to upgrade to the higher priced Botticelli by providing a better product supported by consistent

TV advertising that explains to consumers why the product is superior in every way, and why it will make for a better and more memorable mealtime.

While the trade-up model is easy to understand, I feel it necessary to explain the trade-down model and why no buyer wants to add these items. Every so often, we will get a call from a CPG company that is extremely excited to tell us all about their new, low-price leading product. Often it will be something like this: "We have come up with a way to produce this product for less money, and we can offer consumers a package with twice as much product that costs 30% less." They then tell us how, "Every retailer will want that."

It falls on us to tell them that no retailer except maybe some dollar stores will have any interest in their product. The problem is they just reduced the retailers' margin by 30% and by making the product in a larger volume, they have reduced the replenishment cycle, hurting the retailer even further.

If you really want to be a hero to your mass retail buyer, make a product that is higher-priced and needs to be replenished more often. That is the ultimate one-two punch for retail.

For all these reasons, we nearly always recommend that anyone in the CPG space focuses on innovation, intellectual property, product performance and user experience, not on low pricing.

Model 3: New Money

For the most part, planograms are designed for a specific demographic or group of demographics. For example, energy drinks skew young, while feminine care focuses on women. The categories can be broad or narrower: men's grooming, kids' cough and cold and diabetic skin care, for example. You get the idea. A "new money" model is when your product has the ability to reach into a new demographic which results in more and new people coming to that planogram. In other words, you are getting people to shop in this section of the store who previously did not shop there.

Let's go back to energy drinks and their consumer model. Energy drinks tend to go after a youth consumer with names like *Monster*, *Red Bull* and *Venom*. Now, let's assume for a moment that you have developed a new energy drink that is for adults 55 and over and has a strong advertising campaign behind it to drive sales. This has a great chance of getting into retail since you are not cannibalizing sales for any of the existing brands but would be bringing consumers from a new demographic to the category. No smart retail buyer will bring in a new product if all it will do is take the same sales dollars of the current assortment and divide them across an additional item.

A few years back, we had a client come in that was struggling at retail. It was a single SKU shaving cream called Cremo. What we noticed is that the women in our office loved it for shaving, raving about how much smoother, slicker and better it was than any of the shaving cream in the women's shaving section.

From that insight, we launched a radio campaign aimed at women. We told women how it was just wrong that men's products all worked better than the best women's product. This was a universal truth that women were all too happy to agree with.

The ad went on to tell women about Cremo shave cream—about how impossibly slick it is and how women were discovering it in the men's section of the store. Immediately, women across America started going to the men's aisle looking for the product, bringing new money to the shelf and resulting in nearly every retailer in the country bringing in the product line.

You may be asking yourself; didn't we steal sales from the women's section in the very same store? The answer is yes, but our product sold for a higher price and the buyer of men's care is not the same buyer for women's care. The men's buyer was happy to pull sales from the women's section, since he gets paid for what his department sells, not anyone else's.

For clarification, each department, or "set," in a major retailer operates with its own profit and loss report. Each buyer and category leader is responsible for their own P and L. The stores are designed to place buyers in a friendly competition with each other. So the men's grooming buyer is happy to take money from the women's product buyer if they are not the same person.

Another example of internal competition is that the Health and Beauty department often finds itself in conflict with First Aid. As an example, a skin lotion used for after-sun care could be sold in either place, but chances are only one of the departments is going to get that particular product. This is another lesson on why you need to know every account intimately and have brokers with deep connections inside the organization to help navigate the retailer complexities.

A final thought is: Pay attention to "Whose ox is being gored?" or as Joe Polish says, "What's in it for them?"

Rule 5 Questions

- Which one of the three levers or pathways does your product fit?
- Does it fit more than one?
- What products currently on the shelf can you replace?
- What is the best department and set for your product in each retailer?

RULE 6

NEVER MAKE A PRODUCT THAT CAN'T BE DESCRIBED IN ONE SENTENCE

"Remember you are dealing with temporary people making permanent decisions."
—Chuck Woolery

One of my closest and dearest friends was the late, legendary game show host Chuck Woolery. Chuck was the closest thing to a big brother that I ever had and was a tremendous source of wisdom. Chuck had more hit shows (a total of seven) than nearly anyone else in Hollywood. He really knew the industry.

He and I were working on a new TV series that we were pitching to NBC with another old friend by the name of Bernie Brillstein. Bernie was the manager for almost every cast member in history on *Saturday Night Live*, including Lorne Michaels. You may not know his name, but you have seen him. You see, Bernie was also the manager for Jim Henson, creator of The Muppets. Henson created two curmudgeonly characters (Statler and Waldorf)—the two old men in the balcony that complained about everything during *The Muppet Show*. Bernie was literally the inspiration for the Muppet on the left of the screen. While we were working on the show pitch in Bernie's office, we sat next to a glass case that contained the actual Muppet of Bernie. It was a reminder that we were in the office of one of the most powerful men in all of Hollywood.

Needless to say, these two experienced Hollywood guys knew how to pitch a new show. But even so, they also understood how difficult it is to get a new show greenlit by a network and how important it is to have the right pitch. Keeping us focused, Chuck said, "Never take more than one sentence to describe your project." The point that he was making is that network executives are remarkably busy people being pitched ideas all day long, sometimes even by a barista at the local Starbucks. (In Hollywood, everyone is an aspiring writer or actor.) These network executives get worn out hearing pitches and have short attention spans.

We were tossing around ideas and trying to refine them to make the greatest impact on the network executives, as we knew that the time allotted for the pitch was limited. It was during this time that Chuck (who often boiled down the obvious to simple, folksy one liners that just made a lot of sense), delivered one of his many pearls of wisdom. He expressed our shared frustration when he said we were dealing with "temporary people making permanent decisions."

What he meant was that in the entertainment world, people in talent and acquisition tend to be transient. So the network people we were meeting with not only had the power and were far less vested in our success than we were, but they measured success in the short-term, not long-term. They might be at another network next year, so they are looking for immediate out-of-the-gate success. That means they need a pitch they can easily understand and that they believe can be successful—quickly.

The working title of the new show we were pitching was *The Next Big Thing*. The pitch and show premise was "Inventors and entrepreneurs deliver their best elevator pitch to a three-to-four-person panel of successful businesspeople in hopes of securing a partnership." The idea was to have them think of it as *American Idol* for consumer products.

As you may have figured out by now, that show became *Shark Tank.*

Just as we needed the right pitch for the television network executives, the same is true with retail buyers. Chuck's wisdom about never taking more than one sentence to describe your project was not only spot on for the world of network TV, but it applies beautifully to the CPG world. Retail buyers are seeing new products all day long, and sometimes hear as many as 30 new pitches in a day. Most entrepreneurs are so revved up about the meeting that they cannot contain their enthusiasm to tell the buyer all about themselves, how wonderful the brand is and why people are going to love it. It often takes so long to get to the point that the buyer has already mentally checked out.

These buyers receive endless product pitches from people looking to have them give up some of their precious, limited shelf space. So they need to see quick success. They are focused on the short-term impact. Therefore, there is not much time for us to grow the business.

More specifically, retail buyers do not initially care about sales 36 months from now when it comes to a new product. Instead, their focus is on the first 30 days. No buyer is interested in giving us time to develop on their shelf. They expect us to be a hero from day one.

Because just like people in Hollywood acquisitions, the retail buyers also move on or get replaced. They may be in a different category or even another retailer next year. In that sense, retail buyers are also "temporary people making permanent decisions." While they are in it for the short term, you are in it for the long haul.

Whether it's Hollywood, Bentonville, Arkansas (Walmart),

Woonsocket, Rhode Island (CVS) or some other city where a retailer is headquartered, you must remember that the people you encounter will have nowhere near your level of passion for your product, nor will they have the emotional and financial investment in it that you do.

Your product, no matter how wonderful or extensive, needs to be able to be described in one sentence. There are two rules to follow:

The first rule is the foundation of journalism: who, what, where and how. Not all are critical, but if you follow these tenets and "keep the main thing the main thing" people will understand what you are making.

The second rule is to write the sentence at a seventh-grade reading level. The newspaper *USA Today* is written at a seventh-grade reading level. The average US adult reads at a seventh-to-eighth-grade reading level according to a 2023 study by the Organisation for Economic Co-operation and Development (OECD). The twelfth-grade-reading-level individual has no problem reading the seventh-grade reading level, but not vice versa. If my prime demographic is graduate-school-education-and-above people with luxury income levels, then it may be appropriate to speak to them with graduate-school-and-above language. Otherwise, talk to the broadest audience.

Love him or hate him, President Donald Trump is a master of this concept. *CNN* has done analysis on Trump speeches and reported that he talks at a fifth-grade level. Some believe it is because Donald Trump is not well-educated. In reality, he has an MBA from the Wharton School, the business school of the University of Pennsylvania. What he has done is follow the rules of communicating by speaking at the level that lets him address the most people in his potential audience.

Here are some examples of successful products that can be described in one sentence:

- **DerMend Bruise Lotion.** A premium skin care product formulated to prevent bruising for mature adults.
- **Botticelli Pasta Sauce.** A premium pasta sauce made in Italy from all farm fresh ingredients with no added sugars or preservatives.
- **WaxRx.** An earwax removal kit which provides the same tools and outcomes as systems used in thousands of doctors' offices.

You get the idea now. What is your one-sentence description? It is okay that there is a lot to say about your brand, but what is that one sentence that tells me exactly what you are selling or what problem you are solving?

Rule 6 Questions

- What is your one-sentence product description?
- Can everyone totally understand what you are selling?
- Can consumers understand why they should buy it?
- Does your description make the product compelling and desirable to them?
- Is your product compelling and desirable?

RULE 7

MASS RETAILERS NEED PRODUCTS THAT APPEAL TO THE MASSES

"High volume leads to low costs. Low costs lead to low prices. And low prices lead to high volume."
—Sam Walton

In retail, we divide the landscape up as F/D/M and C/S/C. FDM is *Food, Drug, Mass* while CSC is *Club, Specialty, Convenience.* If you happen to be selling bottled water, then yes, your product fits everywhere. But notwithstanding something this universal, chances are your product does not fit every retailer.

Imagine the world of retail as a large funnel. At the very top of the funnel are items used by everyone, such as toothpaste, soap, toilet paper or food; you get the idea. As we move a little further down the funnel, we get to items that still appeal to the masses but not everyone. Examples of those items would be feminine care and men's grooming.

As we go further, we get to more specialty items, like baby food, bowling balls, pickleball racquets and espresso machines. A little further down are designer clothing and handbags, premium perfumes and high-end foods.

Then, as we get further down into specialties, we find things like home improvement, pet supplies, tools, automotive after-market products and others.

It is important that you have a complete understanding of which retailers are best suited for your products. You need to do the homework and know this up front. Start by making sure your product truly is a mass product. Look up your category and competitors in databases like *Nielsen* and *IRI* and establish that your category is indeed large enough to appeal to mass retailers. Not only must you understand this, but you also need to know what place in their store you belong. This is not as easy as it sounds sometimes. You need to start by visiting every store you think you belong in, studying the current assortment, then figuring out where you fit in and how you will make the store more money.

You need to be ready to advise the buyers where your product belongs based on where you can sell the most products. And no, you are not likely to get your product on two different category store shelves unless you are a big, established brand.

There are some rare exceptions. Take our client DerMend Bruise Cream. There was originally controversy over where it fit in the store. The first aid buyer felt it belonged in their section since healing a bruise is first aid, but the skin care buyer also made a good argument that it belonged in the beauty section. In the case of DerMend, the product did in fact make sense for both beauty and first aid since there really are two separate consumers that could both desire the product.

Food. Next in line are the big food chains: Walmart, Meijer, Target, Kroger, Albertsons, Publix and HEB. (Although you may think of Walmart, Target and Meijer as general merchandise retailers, they are in fact large-scale grocery retailers, with Walmart holding the number one position.)

Drug. Big chain drug stores are also mass retailers, but not all products fit them. For instance, a chain drug store would not be a good spot for a can opener (even though a can opener is top-of-funnel) because mass drug retailers sell more health care and convenience.

Mass. If you are looking at mass retail, like Walmart, Target or Meijer (a Midwest chain), your product should be as close to the top of the funnel as possible. If your product is not top-of-funnel but is more niche in nature, mass players may not be your first choice.

Club. We then get to club stores—those retailers that have an annual membership fee, such as Costco, Sam's Club and BJ's. Clubs tend to move a massive amount of product. These stores run at the slimmest margins (something like 17% gross margin) since they also have the revenue from those memberships. While a Walmart store carries 148,000 different SKUs, a Costco store may only have 4,000 single SKUs.

Club stores typically only carry the products that have sales that are in the top three in the category. They also do a lot of seasonal buys and configure everything into a higher-volume value package.

As an example, an item at Walmart could be required to sell $40 per store per week to hold onto their shelf space. That same product, albeit in a larger packaged configuration, will need to do nearly $900 per week per store to satisfy Costco's required volume.

Department Stores. Now let's look at department stores like Nordstrom, Neiman Marcus, JCPenney, Macy's and other such stores that are categorized as "mass" but have fewer offerings than a Walmart or Target. These stores tend to be fashion heavy with some housewares and travel. But even this class of trade is very much divided up by pricing, so it is important to pay attention to the pricing and demographic that each of these stores operate in. For example, while Nordstrom can sell $1,000 ladies handbags all day long, JCPenney would be hard pressed to sell a purse for more than $80.

Dollar Stores. Also part of "mass," dollar stores, such as Dollar General and Dollar Tree, tend to fill a gap in stores between food, department and convenience. These dollar stores are great if you need to close out some inventory or have a low-cost, high-volume item. However, you would never roll out a high-level or premium product in these stores.

We must always be careful dealing with dollar stores since having your product appear there can diminish the status of your brand.

Specialty Stores. These stores cover a wide variety of retailers, such as Home Depot, Lowe's, Dick's Sporting Goods, Cabela's, PetSmart and Office Depot. These types of stores are very category-specific, such as sports, home improvement, office supplies, hunting and fishing and pets, so your product would need to be very category-aligned with them in most cases.

Brand-Captured. Another more defined type of specialty store is brand-captured stores. These stores are purposely built to sell a specific line or brand of product. Occasionally they will carry companion products that are not their brand but are made to enhance or blend with their brand. Examples of these stores include Apple, Nike, Lululemon, Tiffany, Tommy Bahama and more.

Convenience. Finally, we have convenience stores, which are also referred to as "C-stores." These are your 7-Elevens, Circle K, Wawa, Speedway and other gas station-based locations. Part of the appeal of these stores is that they are often located in an area that fills a gap between other retailers. They are typically easy to get in and out of, parking is close and they have short lines. They tend to offer convenience-based food, beverages, grab-and-go items and other impulse items.

C-stores are not viable for most products. But just as you

make larger configurations for club stores, sometimes smaller configurations work for C-stores, such as a single serving versus an eight-pack or how Tylenol has tear-open packs with two tablets in them.

As you can see, there is a wide variety of categories and stores. It is on you to know what stores make sense and where your product belongs and where it does not. In addition to this, not only do you need to know what part of the store you belong in, it is also up to you to provide clear recommendations and rationale as to why that is the case. You need to be able to make a case to the retail buyer about why consumers will seek your product out in that specific location.

A good rule of thumb for identifying as a mass product is: You appeal to a minimum of 10-20% of US households. Emerging brands must prove they are mass viable and demonstrate the ability to reach 20-30 million households. Shelf space is scarce. Every new item brought in must displace a current SKU. Retail buyers want to have safe bets, so they don't look at penetration as much as they look at units per store per week. If a $15 product is not moving two to three units per store per week, it is non-sustainable at mass.

Niche products, products that appeal to 7% or less of the population, are better suited for fine, specialty or natural/health stores or online channels.

Rule 7 Questions

- How close to the top of the funnel is your product?
- What are the prime retailers for your product?
- Does your product fit into more than one category of retail?
- How can you reconfigure your product to fit other categories of retail?

RULE 8

IT DOESN'T MATTER WHAT YOUR PRODUCT CAN DO, ONLY WHAT YOU'RE ALLOWED TO SAY IT CAN DO

"There is no greater agony than bearing an untold story inside you."
—Maya Angelou

Just because you have created a new product that gets amazing results (especially health claims), it does not mean you can tell anyone about it. Take as an example our client Heliocare. This is an amazing product developed in Spain that has dozens of clinical studies. In studies, we see that Heliocare mops up free radicals caused by UV exposure that cause skin cancer. Amazing, right? You would think that the government would want everyone to take this product.

But in the eyes of the FDA, this product feature does not exist because it has not been approved as a drug, and therefore cannot claim to treat, cure or prevent any known disease, period. The only way to make these claims would be to spend hundreds of millions of dollars and many years on testing to get it approved as a drug.

Occasionally someone will ask me why supplement manufacturers do not go through the FDA approval process, thinking that even if it cost millions to accomplish, it would be worth it since you then would be able to make drug-like claims. However, beyond the investment in the approval, the common reason is that most supplement ingredients are natural (meaning they exist in nature) and thus cannot be patented—at least not to a point where there is real protection. So, a company that does the monograph work would be at a massive disadvantage since they make the financial investment, but then any other maker could produce the product under the same monograph.

This is why we say it doesn't matter what your product does, only what you can tell people it does.

For many people in the CPG world, you are making a product that we would refer to as a consumable. These, along with some medical devices, are products that make certain claims or promises, whether they be health claims or some type of specified performance.

You cannot go out and make such claims without the necessary backup or you will find yourself on the wrong side of the table from agents of the FDA/FTC/USDA and other three- and four-letter agencies. If this is your class of trade, it is vital that you have a qualified FDA/FTC attorney on your team. Your lawyer should review all of your claims and communications including packaging, website and all advertising copy.

First let's break down the way the government sees products. There are pharmaceuticals, supplements, cosmetics, functional food and beverage, non-functional food and beverage, devices and homeopathy.

Pharmaceuticals. These are products that are intended to diagnose, treat, cure or prevent disease. Drugs are strictly regulated by the FDA and must go through clinical trials and gain pre-market approvals.

An approved drug has a monograph, which spells out exactly what claims can be made for the drug. Examples would be "lowers blood pressure," "reduces anxiety" or "induces sleep."

Both prescription and over-the-counter drugs have monographs. So, legally you could have a product that does not have a monograph and add a monograph product into the formula at the minimum effective dose (MED) and make the claims for that drug under the FDA monograph.

This is much more common than you may think. The product emu oil provides good relief for many consumers suffering with arthritis and joint or muscle pain. However, emu oil does not have a drug monograph so the makers cannot claim that it is a pain-relieving product. But add in some menthol or capsaicin, which do have monographs, and now you can claim pain relief even though the emu oil is really the ingredient that is providing the outcome.

But as I explained earlier, no one is ever going to spend millions of dollars to have emu oil registered as a monograph drug because it is a common product that cannot be protected.

Supplements. These can go anywhere from letter vitamins like A, B, C, D, E and K and expand into more exotic formulations. These products are regulated as food, not drugs, under the DSHEA (Dietary Supplement Health and Education Act of 1994). No FDA preapproval is needed, but manufacturers must ensure safety and accuracy of labeling.

You cannot make drug claims for supplements; you can only make what is called a structure/function claim. For example, "supports bone health" or "supports healthy blood pressure." You cannot claim to treat or diagnose any known disease. That will quickly get you in trouble.

As most of us know in this business, there are many supplements on the market that have drug-like effects on the body. Even if you know this, have run clinical trials and have third-party evidence, without a drug monograph, you are still limited to structure/function claims.

You cannot tell people it can replace their medications and/or that they will be cured of a disease. You could not say that your supplement treats anxiety. You could say that in a clinical trial, 83% of participants reported feeling more relaxed and less anxious. Or that there is data showing that this particular substance may help people feel more relaxed or less anxious. The words we use in advertising are very important. You'll note that the previous sentence said the product "may help" not that it "would help." You must use extreme caution in your advertising language to avoid trouble.

Cosmetics. These are products intended to beautify, cleanse or alter appearances (such as reducing the appearance of fine lines). But these products cannot claim to treat skin conditions unless they contain a registered drug.

Functional food. This is about food items that provide benefits beyond basic nutrition, potentially helping reduce disease or the risk of it, or support body function. These items are treated as food, not drugs, so claims must comply with FDA food labeling laws.

Examples would be yogurt with probiotics, oatmeal for heart health or orange juice with added vitamin D. The health claims for these products are limited to things like "may reduce the risk" but only if significant scientific agreement exists, and proper disclaimers are included. Again, this is another gray area and the reason you need a good lawyer on your team.

At-home medical devices. This breaks into two areas: one is that of measurement or reporting, and the other is of function. For measuring, it is devices used to diagnose, prevent or monitor a health condition or function. This class would include thermometers, blood pressure devices and ECG monitors. You can make claims based on what they do but will need scientific backup as to the accuracy of the device.

As for function, these are devices like red light therapy, PEMF (pulsed electromagnetic field) or TENS (transcutaneous electrical nerve stimulator) units. These devices occupy a complex area because they can be marketed as wellness tools, medical devices or even cosmetic devices. This all depends on claims and how they are classified.

As an example, there are red light masks that help with fine lines—a cosmetic claim—but blue light masks are sold to clear up acne—a medical claim.

If the product is intended to make a medical claim, it will need a 510(k) clearance from the FDA. As an example, a red-light therapy device for pain relief could say, "Temporary relief of muscle and joint pain. Improves circulation, reduces inflammation for minor injuries." The FDA classifies these devices and claims into three categories known as I, II and III.

Unless you have specific 510(k) approvals, you should stick to structure/function claims similar to supplements or wellness claims. Finally, remember that if you use testimonials in your ads, you are responsible for what the person says. So if the testimonial user claims they quit taking prescription meds due to the device, that will be the same as *you* saying that.

On most everything that does not have a drug monograph but is making any kind of health or wellness statement, you should be adding in, "*This product is not intended to diagnose, treat, cure or prevent any disease and has not been reviewed by the FDA.*" We have all heard that phrase in advertising and I offer it up as a reminder only—not as legal advice. As mentioned previously, you need a good lawyer on your team when it comes to claims about your product. If you have a device with a 510(k), which is a premarket submission made to the FDA, your approach can be different. Your attorney can tell you more about that.

Homeopathy. This category occupies a very specific space. Homeopathy was carved out in 1938, when the FDA was first created. It was a protection for doctors that, prior to the FDA's existence, used to compound and make their own treatments.

Many people often confuse homeopathic for organic, natural or supplements; it is none of these. Homeopathy is appraised as drugs by the FDA.

The claimed science (which is often disputed) is that elements that can harm or kill you can also treat you if used in tiny amounts. These harmful molecules or drugs are delivered in the preparation in near-subatomic or unmeasurable quantities. It is for this reason that many argue that homeopathy is quack science.

As I said earlier, homeopathic products are considered drugs by the FDA, but they do not require prior approval provided the claims match up with the allowable standards set in the HPUS (Homeopathic Pharmacopeia of the United States).

Because this guide dates back to 1938, you will find that many medical diagnoses of today do not exist in it. An example would be restless leg syndrome. This was not a known disease state in 1938. Therefore, there is no homeopathic treatment for it.

If your product falls under this classification, you want to pay the strictest of attention to your formulations and your claims. Although the level and intensity of enforcement by the FDA/FTC can vary from one administration to the next, homeopathy gets a lot of scrutiny due to the belief by many that it is pseudoscience.

It's important for you to do the homework and understand what category and class of trade you fall into. If you are struggling to define it, this is a great time to rely on your whos, i.e., attorney, formulator, broker and ad agency.

Note: You may notice a lot of online brands making outrageous claims. Maybe even you are making outrageous claims. Understand that the internet is a vast, open Wild West environment that the FDA and FTC have a difficult time policing, especially new startups. However, once you move into the big world (brick-and-mortar retail), you are now on their radar. You can quickly run into trouble with consumer complaints that trigger investigations and fines. Additionally, the biggest retailers and major advertising sources will likely ask you for claims substantiation on your product. If your product can't tell the truth and survive online, it is probably not going to get into or survive the truth required in brick-and-mortar.

Rule 8 Questions

- If your product falls into the health and wellness category, what classification does it fit into?
- Do you need to consider adding in a monographed drug to make your performance claims?
- Have all of your claims been reviewed and approved in writing by a qualified FDA/FTC lawyer?

RULE 9

NEVER BE THE LOW-PRICE LEADER; BE THE MOST EXPENSIVE IN YOUR CATEGORY

"Make your product so good, people feel proud to pay a premium."
—Seth Godin

Why not be the low-price leader? Surely that has appeal to many consumers, right? Well, to start with, in the CPG world, you can never be the low-price leader because someone from China or a private-label store brand will always beat you on price. You will lose a race to the bottom. So, your options are to be in the middle of the pack or at the top of the pricing scale.

For the most part, there is not a lot of value in being the middle product, but like anything else, there are always exceptions to the rule. One exception would be if you are in a category that has what we call "massclusive" offerings. These are typically categories like food, spirits, fashion and beauty.

Examples of "massclusive" products are Coach handbags. They have brand cachet, are certainly more expensive than a handbag from Walmart or Target, but they are considerably less than a high-end bag such as a Gucci or Louis Vuitton. A Walmart bag can be $15 to $25 and a Coach or Michael Kors handbag would be $150 to $300, but a Gucci or Louis Vuitton can easily be $3,000-plus.

Brands like Coach or Michael Kors are what we refer to as aspirational brands. These are brands for consumers that want more and desire the prestige of ownership but are not in the real premium space.

An even bigger gap for example is wristwatches, devices that no matter what, still have the same primary function of telling time. You can buy a Timex or Casio watch for $15 to $30 dollars, or a tech watch from Apple for $300 or upgrade to a Seiko and spend $400. But what if you go to Movado or Tag Heuer? Now you are spending $3,000. But what if you decide Rolex or Breitling is for you? Now you are spending $10,000 to $30,000, with six-figure options available.

Remember that other than some complications like stop-watches and day/date, watches all do the same thing. Now, let's say those previously listed watches are all just too run of the mill for you, so you decide you would like to own a Richard Mille. You are now spending between $330,000 and $2,000,000 for a single wristwatch.

As Godin indicated in the quotation above, people are proud of paying more. The reason someone will pay a million dollars for a Richard Mille watch is simple; they really love the artistry of it, but even more important, they buy it because they can. It makes them a part of an exclusive club. The watch is so exclusive that you cannot even buy one at a Richard Mille store; you can only look at them and then pay to get onto a waiting list. (Unless you are Sly Stallone, then you call Richard personally and you get your watch.) The reality is, it is so rare that most people would not even know what a Richard Mille watch is, or its value. But for the owner of such a watch, the people who matter to them will know.

You can make an item, like a watch, that on the surface has broad appeal, but in reality does not appeal to everyone. (In fairness, this may also indicate that I know way too much about fine timepieces.)

Another thing to note is that volume isn't everything. Rolex sold one million watches in 2022 for a company topline number of 9.7 billion dollars. Timex, on the other hand, is the world's number one seller of watches by unit count, with annual sales of 1.4 billion dollars. Which brand would you rather own?

ROLEX	TIMEX
2022 1 MILLION UNITS SOLD $9.7 Billion	2022 WORLD'S #1 BY UNITS/ANNUAL SALES $1.4 Billion

The point is that every category of trade has a basic demographic base, and inside that base are the more refined subbases which are specific to each brand. Also, we need to recognize that these bases can move up and down the scale. All Neiman Marcus shoppers can buy from Target; however, not all Target shoppers can afford to shop at Neiman's.

It is important to know who your customer base is, otherwise you will not know how to efficiently advertise and market to them. Some conclusions are obvious, like: It would make little sense to market Rolex to a low-income worker. But not all price differences have to be such large numbers to still impact sales and profitability.

Pricing differences make sense in several categories. For example, in pasta sauces there is Ragú at $1.99 versus Botticelli at $4.99 versus Rao's at $7.99. It is interesting that there is enormous room in the market for all three brands to do well. That said, you want to be at the top of the pricing model. To demonstrate the value of this, Rao's was recently sold to Campbell's Soup Company for $2.7 billion.

Where do you want to be in your pricing? First, let's look at the value of being a premium product versus a competitive product. As a rule, there is a 10x difference between the cheapest item in a category and the costliest. That means that if the cheapest product in a category sells for $0.99, the best one in the class sells for around $10. As you can see, there is a lot of price flexibility in most classes of trade.

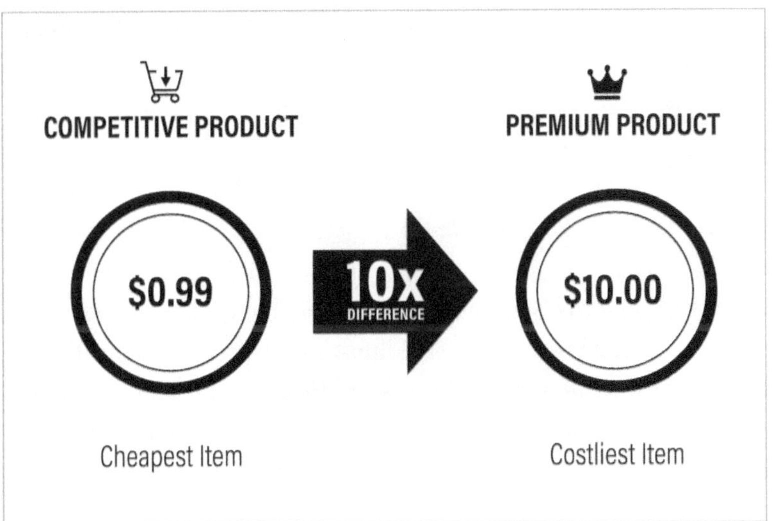

Now, here is the shocker; it costs about four times more to manufacture the highest-priced item versus the lowest. This means that the higher-priced product has far more margin and profit, which in turn means the better brands can advertise more. If you start noticing advertising, you will find that in CPG, it is rarely the lowest priced item advertised, because there is no margin for it.

Many new clients come to us with a low-price strategy. Their thinking is they can make a similar or even better product that will be lower priced than a leading brand, or they will provide a large quantity of the product making it a better deal.

No retailer wants this product!

Why? Let's break this down. Imagine you are the buyer at a major retailer; you have a limited amount of shelf space and any new product you add to your assortment means you must remove some other item.

A new vendor comes to you and says, "I have a better product than Product X and I cost two dollars less." As the retail buyer, you are being asked if you want to reduce the sale of one item and sell a different item for less money. This means less margin to the retailer and taking up two shelf spaces to do what you are currently doing with just one. This is a losing strategy for the retailer.

Another thought process of a new vendor is thinking, "We can match Product X's price but give the customer more product, perhaps 20%-plus more product for the same price." Now the retail buyer is being asked to sell each customer fewer units per year since you have given them more product, resulting in less profit for the retailer. This is not beneficial for the retailer.

The pricing strategy that best works with every major retailer is simply this: a premium product, with a higher price and higher profit margin, that has a genuine point of difference or superiority. Now, add in supporting that product with an advertising campaign that will drive traffic to the stores and product from the shelf. That is the clear winner and one that retail buyers will embrace.

On rare occasions, there are products that have no competitor, which changes pricing strategy. An example is: In 1997, the KAO Corp, through its US company Jergens, came out with a new product called Bioré Pore Strips. This is an adhesive strip you place on your nose, leave on for a few minutes and tear off. Left on the strip are all the disgusting blackheads, whiteheads and other material from inside your pores. This made for an amazing visual that shocked consumers when they realized that the skin on their nose contained all of this disgusting matter. KAO ran an aggressive TV campaign showing the strips after use.

Not only was it compelling, but Bioré had zero competition in this category as they were the first to market with this product. They did not need to adjust their pricing based on other products; they only needed to price the product against the perceived value to the consumer. In other words, what would the average person be willing to pay to remove all this gross material from their skin? In this particular case, it allowed Bioré to have a massive markup that was probably 20x cost of goods, making the product an enormous success and wildly profitable.

However, there is a dark side to outsized profits and market share. Any time a company has oversized or large profits, it attracts a lot of knockoffs and competitors. Other companies cannot resist the urge to jump into a category with massive profits. Assuming the profits are big enough, many firms will jump in even though they know they are risking violating your patent.

If you are lucky enough to have a totally unique and unchallenged product, congratulations. But know that this too will end, as you will attract future competitors and you will need to know how to run your company on traditional margins in the future.

Rule 9 Questions

- How close to the top of the pricing scale is your product?
- Does your product bring more profit to a retailer?
- Can you demonstrate to your buyer how your product is a trade-up alternative?

RULE 10

NEVER HAVE LESS THAN A FIVE TO ONE MARGIN

"If they ask you why your price is so high, tell them, 'I am not selling a product; I am selling the results.'"
—Mark Young

Many of my new clients are curious as to why one of the first questions we ask them is, "What is the cost of your goods and what is their price point?" The reason we ask this is because all too often, we find brands in their early stages do not charge enough for their product in order to make a profit and stay in business. We frequently hear things like, "We have a 40% or 50% margin!" from brands who think this will carry them to success.

There are many, many factors that will affect how you price your product. The traditional way that pricing is determined is called cost plus. This is when we first calculate the "all-in landed cost." This means: What does it cost to make one item and land it in your warehouse?

Continuing with this model, we then look for a markup of at least five times the original price, but preferably eight times if possible. I know that some people think this sounds too high, but let's walk through the numbers.

Let's say that our product's landed cost is $4, making it at least a $20 retail-priced item. Now, most retailers will be looking for a 43% to 50% margin, so using the 43%, our wholesale price is $11.40.

```
LANDED COST:  $4.00
5X MARK UP:    $20.00
```

```
$20.00  RETAIL PRICE
- $8.60  43%  Margin
─────────────────────────
$11.40  WHOLESALE PRICE
.........................

$11.40  WHOLESALE PRICE
- $0.92  8%   Master Broker
- $0.57  5%   Trade Marketing
- $0.34  3%   Damage + Returns
- $2.85  25% Advertising Budget
─────────────────────────
$6.72   NET PER UNIT
- $4.00  Cost of Goods
─────────────────────────
$2.72 = PROFIT
```

Assuming we have a master broker working for us, they will get 8% or $0.92 per unit. Now we are down to $10.48.

We will need to account for trade marketing, which will be in the area of 5%, or $0.57 per unit. Damage and returns should be estimated at $3, or $0.34 per unit. Finally, our advertising budget will likely be 15% in the long term but closer to 25% to 30% in the short term. Let's use the 25% number, which is $2.85.

So now, let's look at the math: $20 retail minus costs (-43% margin, -8% broker, -5% trade marketing, -3% damage, -25% advertising budget) equals $6.72 net profit per unit. Subtracting your $4 cost of goods leaves you with $2.72 to run a business and earn a profit. This does not take into account any extraordinary cost, such as a markdown, R and D or if a retail account requires a slotting fee.

I know this can be sobering. But let's stay with it.

The next thing we need to look at is: What is the going rate for your class of trade? As an example, if the highest priced product is $10 and you are at $20 for the same item due to your cost of goods, we can probably assume your cost of goods is too high and we need to figure out how to lower your manufacturing cost.

There are exceptions to this rule, however. There are conditions that will allow you to sell into a market at 10 or 20 times the highest priced item in the class. One of our clients, WaxRx, sells a $40 item in a market that averages $8 per good, so they are literally five times the price of the premium product. The reason is that WaxRx is not really in competition with other earwax removers; instead, it is competing with a trip to the doctor.

The Wrong Comparison (Retail Shelf)

$8.00 Average Ear Wax Remover

$40.00 WaxRx Kit

The Real Competition (Convenience/Healthcare Cost)

$40.00 WaxRx Kit

$100.00 Doctor Visit - *Appointments, Copays, Treatments, Time*

We know that no one is going to flop down $40 when there is an $8 solution on the shelf. But by drilling down into the customers' needs, we know that there is a decent percentage of consumers for whom the $8 solution fails, and they are left going to a doctor's office.

WaxRx is made by the same people that make the kits used in the doctor's office, but this product is designed for use at home. So, simply put, we are not trying to convert $8 buyers; we are saving people from time off work and a doctor visit.

This also meets the needs of the retailer since we take no business away from the other items on the shelf. We are the solution to step up to once those products fail, meaning the retailer just got a sale using dollars that typically have gone to a doctor.

There are many opportunities in the marketplace like this. Waterpik is one example that offers a solution beyond brushing and flossing. Another example is the blue light office-like dental tooth-whitening systems. The same holds true in beauty and hair care with salon products.

Rule 10 Questions

- What is the bottom and top pricing of your category?
- Are you at a minimum five to one markup?
- Are there ways to lower your cost of goods?
- Are you competing with the other items in your category or are you really expanding the consumers' at-home options?

RULE 11

ONE SUCCESSFUL ITEM IS BETTER THAN 10 MEDIOCRE PRODUCTS

"One home run is much better than two doubles."
—Steve Jobs

There is an almost universal trend amongst inventors and entrepreneurs to start inventing the next product as soon as they get finished with the last one. Everyone is under the assumption that they need to have a product line in order to get into retail and to be successful. This is simply not true.

Here's what is true:

- Creating multiple products from the start is more distraction than benefit. Having multiple products puts a strain on cash flow, since you must pay for multiple inventories.
- Multiple products up front make you run the risk of expired product since not all units will be equal.
- Multiple products mean multiple advertising campaigns which most startup or early-stage companies cannot support.

- Multiple products, if presented to retailers, can result in a terribly bifurcated retail landscape. This means you present four items to retailers and have to deal with their decisions. Retailer A may decide to take Product One, while Retailer B wants Product Two and Retailer C selects Product Three or Four. Now you have three or four different items in distribution and no hope of running an effective advertising campaign for all of them.

An example of an exception to the multiple products issue would be if CVS took a four-ounce unit and Walmart carries a two-ounce, but it is the exact same product and packaging, just a size difference.

Here is the other reason one item is better than multiple items when starting out; with exceedingly rare exceptions, no retailer is going to say "yes" to multiple SKUs from a new or untested brand. Shelf space is far too valuable to risk more than one slot on an unproven product.

There is an old rule known as Pareto's law or principle. Pareto states that 80% of consequences come from 20% of causes. It is a form of power-law distribution and is commonly called the 80/20 rule. It is not always exactly 80/20, but sometimes 90/10 or 70/30. The point is, that imbalance is more commonplace than most people realize.

It is not unusual for us to speak to a growing company with a dozen or more SKUs. When we ask them to review the numbers, they usually find that 80% to 90% of their current revenue comes from a single item. That's the hero.

Your best chance at success is to make one hero product and put everything you have behind it. That hero item becomes your sole focus. Trying to fight a war on several fronts at once is a bad strategy (think WWII Germany). That thought is the perfect segue to the next rule about cannibalizing your hero.

Rule 11 Questions

- Have you identified your hero product?
- What percentage of your current sales (if any) are from the hero?

RULE 12

DON'T CANNIBALIZE YOUR HERO PRODUCT

"I would rather have four quarters than 100 pennies."
—Al Capone

It takes way more work to get your first product into major retail than it will your next one. Think of Newton's first law of motion, also known as the law of inertia. A thing in motion tends to stay in motion until it is impacted by an outside source. The point is that it takes much more energy or work to get an object moving than it does to keep it moving. Once you have a product that is moving, don't derail it. Keep it going.

Be aware that once you have a hero item that is making retailers money, they will be asking you what else you have. They will want to know what the next item is from you that could make them money. While it sounds exciting, it can be a dangerous time.

A common mistake made by many brands is to make multiple versions of the current item. As an example, we had an excellent mint mouthwash on the market that was doing great numbers. When the retailer asked for the next product, this marketer decided they would introduce two new flavors: cinnamon and wintergreen.

What happened was a near disaster. They did not expand their customer base by adding flavors, because no one was passing them by based on the mint flavor. Their loyal customer base then divided their purchases between the three SKUs, which meant all of the SKUs were now underperforming. In fact, the total sales of the three SKUs combined started to go down compared to previous sales of the one flavor.

This is known as the paradox of choice; the more options you give a consumer, the more they second-guess their own decisions and buy nothing. This was a famous test done by Smucker's years back. Smucker's put live product demonstrators into grocery stores. They offered customers a free sample of grape and strawberry jelly. On average, 50% of the time, a taster bought one of the two flavors.

Then Smucker's introduced a third, fourth and more flavors. Every time they added another option, the total number of sales went down. Faced with too many options, consumers struggled to decide and simply bought less.

If you do not have a second *unique* SKU, your business will actually benefit more from you telling the buyer that you have nothing new this year than it will if you give them a new product that cannibalizes your current one. This can be a difficult internal battle. Your heart and ego may tell you that another SKU would mean you now have a product line in retail instead of a single product, and that you are on your way to greater successes. I must caution you to resist the temptation.

Brand Extensions

When we are looking to expand a product line, we must first always protect the hero. We only consider risking the hero if we have developed a new and improved product that will grossly outperform the hero, even if it will cannibalize it.

What we want to develop is a brand extension using the brand as a leverage point. We need to ask, "How can we bring our loyal customers deeper into our universe?" Going back to our mouthwash example, the brand pivoted away from multiple flavors and instead expanded into indications. This meant they moved to special formulas for dry mouth and another for gingivitis. This brought new consumers to the brand who identified with the indication-specific solution as opposed to a general mouthwash solution.

To effectively leverage your brand while not damaging your hero, you need to lean into indication versions, companion products, value propositions or function claims.

Indication Versions

For many CPG products in the health space, indications is an easy leverage point to expand your brand. Studies show that about 78% of consumer health decisions on health items are based on the indication. A couple examples of indication-specific product campaigns that we designed were mouthwash for 55-plus-year-olds and repackaging a topical pain cream as a back pain formula.

The ultimate example is Robitussin. When I recently asked an AI engine how many different formulas there are, it responded that it was impossible to track them all. Go to your drug store shelf and look at the cough aisle. There will be 10-plus versions including: Cough, Flu + Sore Throat formula, Nighttime CoughDM, Cough + Chest CongestionDM, 12-hour Cough + Mucus Relief, Honey Nighttime CoughDM, Day & Night Value Pack, Severe Cough + Sore Throat, as well as Long-Acting Cough Gels, Soft Chews, hemorrhoid (not really, just wanted to see if you are paying attention) and a variety of children's versions.

And guess what? We are all guilty of shopping this way. Think of the last time you bought a cough product; you read the labels for the version that best suited your symptoms. By making these products for specific indications, they have pushed out many competitors because consumers want to buy the product that best fits their needs.

Companion Products

Companion products are products that work alongside your hero. Our client Bob Evans Foods is a good example. Their hero product is premade mashed potatoes. This is a hugely popular product. So how did they leverage it without hurting the hero? By introducing Bob Evans macaroni and cheese as well as broccoli and cheese, glazed apples and other side dishes. They created items that did not replace the mashed potatoes. They made items you could serve in addition to the mashed potatoes.

Our client WaxRx, the number one earwax removal system in America, just rolled out their newest item: EarAche Rx for ear pain. This is again leveraging the brand while not cannibalizing the hero.

Value Propositions

The value proposition is exactly what it sounds like. Going back to Bob Evans, they have had the family-sized package of mashed potatoes, knowing that people also have the product for family meals and large gatherings. But they also took the mashed potatoes and made dual-pack single servings, knowing they had a lot of seniors buying the product who needed something smaller.

Another advantage to the multiple-size idea is to fit the size to the retailer. Our client RectiCare makes a premium hemorrhoid product that sells for around $30 in the drug channel. This is at the higher end of the price point for Walmart, so rather than lower the price for Walmart, they made a half-size tube that sells for $16.99.

On the other end of the spectrum are the club stores where they focus on large value packs. You would think that there is a limited market for a jar of peanut butter that can hold the average cat, but those jars are sold every day in club stores. Package size is how you fit the club store model while not attacking your base mass retailers and your hero product.

Functional Claims

Last are functional claims. These are similar to an indication but not the same. Returning to our Bob Evans example, they created Bob Evans Naturals. These were made with non-GMO organic potatoes and no chemicals or preservatives. Again, this allows them to leverage the brand but add additional market share by appealing to the vegan and the organic shopper.

Function claims can come in all kinds of different configurations including no seed oil, no sugar, non-GMO, organic, added vitamins and natural food coloring. With the current MAHA (Make America Healthy Again) movement, these issues are becoming top-of-mind and present unlimited numbers of opportunities.

Retailers today want to know that brands ultimately have multi-SKU capabilities. But it is not necessarily needed during the first time in store. Additionally, they will be looking for new SKUs that do not cannibalize the hero SKU.

Rule 12 Questions

- Are you protecting your hero?
- How can you leverage your hero into other products without taking sales away from it?
- How can you reach new customers or increase your current customer's cart size?

PART II

INVESTMENT STRATEGIES

RULE 13

BE THE BIGGEST SPENDER ON ADVERTISING AS A PERCENTAGE OF SALES

"The business that can afford to spend the most to acquire a customer wins."
—Dan Kennedy

There is more money lost every year by businesses underspending on advertising than has ever been lost by overspending. Before you start to panic, I am not saying you need to have the largest advertising campaign or spend the most overall dollars. What I am saying is you need to be the biggest spender in your category, based on your sales.

As Kennedy so correctly states, the brand that spends the most to acquire a new client is the winner. This means you need to budget for being the top spender by percentage. Let me break this down and clarify it.

As an example, say you have a competitor doing 10 million in sales and spending one million on advertising. That means they are spending 10% on advertising. So to outperform them you need to spend a greater percentage of sales.

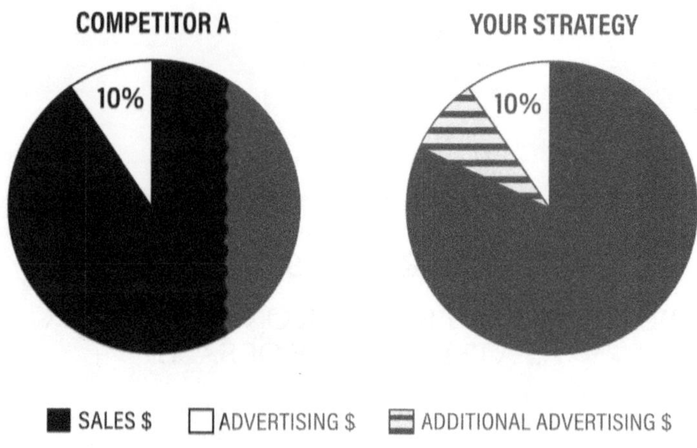

Let's say that your goal run rate for this year is $5 million, and you decide that you will spend 15% of sales compared to their 10%, so your budget is $750,000. You are still spending less in real dollars than your $10 million competitor, but you are outspending them on a per-unit basis. We will cover goal run rate as a multiplier in depth in the next chapter.

This is critical to have rapid growth, and it is the pathway followed by every dominant CPG brand in the market. This is also why premium brands tend to be the most successful—they have more margin to deploy into advertising and customer acquisition.

Keep in mind when we discuss spending the most to acquire a new customer, we need to look at the lifetime value of a new customer, not the one-time, first purchase. If we sell a $20 product but spend $10 on advertising, we think we spent 50% on advertising, but if our customer buys five units per year, we just spent $10 to sell $100, or just 10%. Any rational person would take as much of this business as they can get.

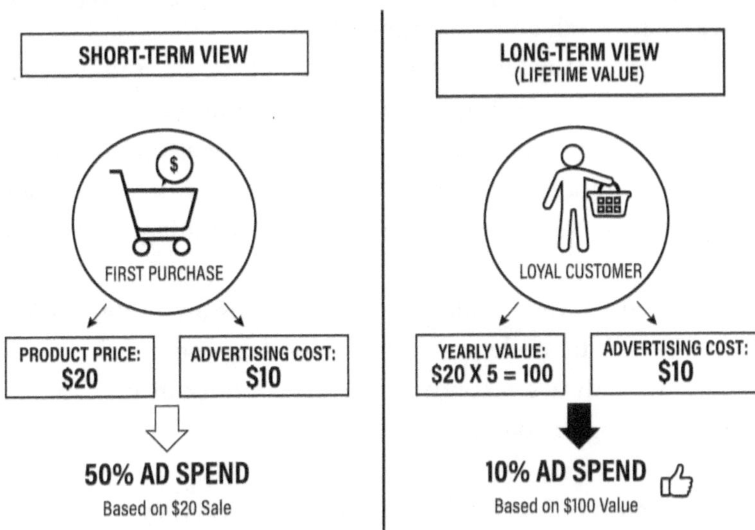

There is another equally important reason to spend the most as a percentage of sales. It is called frequency. The average consumer is being hit with between 6,000 and 25,000 ad impressions each day. This creates incredible clutter and an inability to remember every ad they have been exposed to.

This is where frequency shines. Today we run on something called the "Rule of Seven," which is that a consumer needs to be exposed to a message seven times before they act. Frequency is like compounded interest; the number of sales that happen after a consumer has seen a spot seven-plus times can be as much as 20x of seeing it once.

This is in part a reflection on the fact that the customer purchase journey has gotten longer in some categories. While customers are inundated with media, they have taken more control over their purchase journeys. With the information conveniently available at our fingertips, customers are doing more research and consulting their online tribe (through reviews and social media) and taking more time to move from evaluation to purchase. So the delay is not just going from awareness to consideration anymore, it's getting through the extensive research and evaluation phase.

Now that you understand the need to be the biggest spender on customer acquisition on a per-unit basis, you next need to know how to find out what your competition is spending. This is literally corporate intelligence gathering. You do not want to guess what your competition is spending; you need to know.

There are several data-gathering services available to help you in your intel endeavors. Just know that none of them are perfect, so I always recommend using more than one source and comparing the data.

1. *Kantar*: Subscription-based data service, they track major channels, TV, digital, print, radio and out-of-home (OOH).
2. *Nielsen Ad Intel*: Subscription-based, focus on TV, digital, radio, print and OOH.
3. *Pathmatics*: They provide detailed ad creatives and spending reports with a focus on digital media, social, display and video.
4. *Media Radar*: Tracks creative, spend and media trends with focus on multichannel ad intelligence including B2B, TV, print and digital.
5. *iSpot*: Subscription-based, focus on linear and Connected TV and Over-The-Top services (CTT and OTT), ad spend and performance. Provides real-time tracking of national TV ads.
6. *Standard Media Index*: They pull actual billing data from major ad agencies, covering TV, digital and other paid media.

Rule 13 Questions

- Do you know how big your category is?
- What is the annual ad spend in your category?
- What percentage of sales are your biggest competitors dedicating to advertising?
- What percentage of sales must you dedicate to advertising to outperform them?
- What must you spend to acquire a new customer?
- What is the lifetime value of your average customer?

RULE 14

ADVERTISE BASED ON WHERE YOU WANT TO GO, NOT WHERE YOU'VE BEEN

"What got you here won't get you there."
—Marshall Goldsmith

I must admit, this is one of the most difficult rules for many brand marketers to grasp. My guess is it is due to the nature of traditional accounting practices, which means looking at numbers in the past, not in the future.

The Spend Formula

Let's say that we have examined your category and competitors, and we realize the biggest brands are spending 15% of sales on advertising. Since we want to be the biggest spender in the class—per unit—we decide to go with 17% of sales. So far, so good—but here is where this falls apart for many people. They look at the last year of sales to make the budget. So a brand with $5,000,000 in sales might decide that a 17% ad budget is $850,000. And they would be correct looking backwards (or forward with no growth). However, what if our sales goal for this year is $10,000,000? Then $850,000 is no longer

17% of sales, it is only 8.5% of sales—literally half of what it should be.

When determining the ad budget for the next 12 months, we must first decide on what our sales goal is. Next, we need to determine the percentage of sales needed for the budget to be the biggest spender in the category. Finally, we now apply that percentage over the new sales goal.

For this example, the goal of 17% of $10,000,000 is $1,700,000. This is the budget and how dominant brands plan their future.

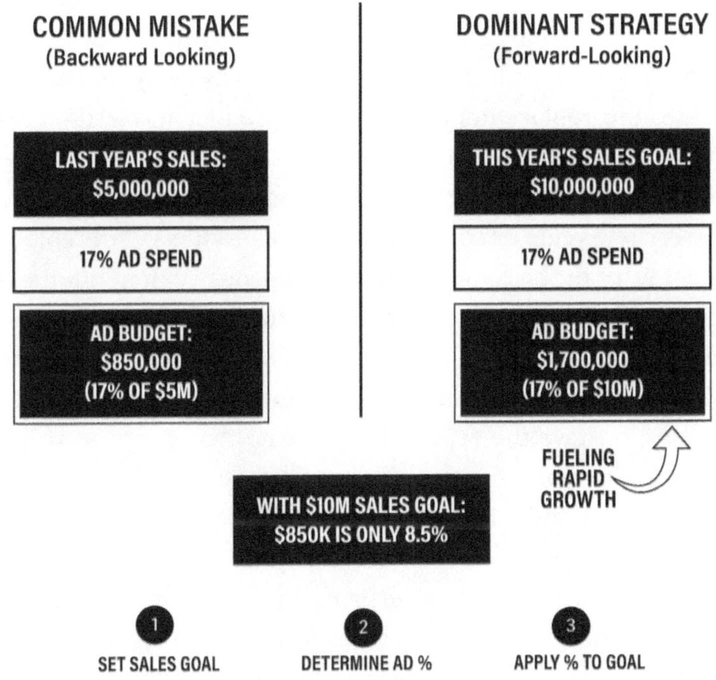

Now keep in mind that these budgets are not cast in concrete. Let's say that mid-year, we gain another major retail account which will have an instantaneous impact on our sales for the year. We need to adjust the ad budget number up. The other side of that equation would be if we lost distribution. An adjustment would be needed to account for this. Another issue that could require an ad budget adjustment is a hiccup on our supply chain, meaning we cannot produce product fast enough.

Other Budget Impactors

First, let's address the obvious: inflation. Inflation hits every-thing, and media is no different. Media for 2024 has averaged a 3% inflation rate, much of that fueled by a 2.5% increase in advertising spending. So, in real terms, you will need to increase your ad budget by roughly 3% just to run in place.

But now let's get to the major reason why budgets have to increase: the replacement rate. Every product has a replace-ment or replenishment cycle. For some products, it is close to zero—like a blender, which is something a consumer may only buy every few years or so. Then there are products with replen-ishment rates in the one-to-two-year category, such as a topical antiseptic, sunscreen or itch cream. At the other end, there are products like beverages or ready-to-eat meal products, such as pasta sauce or prepared side dishes. But even these quick-use items do not have the replenishment rate that you may think since consumers are fickle and like to try new things. Even on the high side, a replenishment rate of 20% would be very high.

The most recognized brand in the world, Coca-Cola, with a five billion dollar annual advertising budget, only sells one to two servings of Coke to 40% of their customer base.

What this means is that every day, you are having to buy new consumers to replace the previous consumer that did not come back and repurchase. I know this is going to get a little in the weeds, but stay with me.

Let's say you currently have a product that sells 1,000,000 pieces per year at $10, which is a $10 million brand. Your current ad budget for this volume is probably $1,000,000 to $1,500,000. You decide to increase your budget in year two by $1,000,000 for a new total of $2,500,000. For the sake of this experiment, we will say that the advertising cost to bring in one new customer is $1.

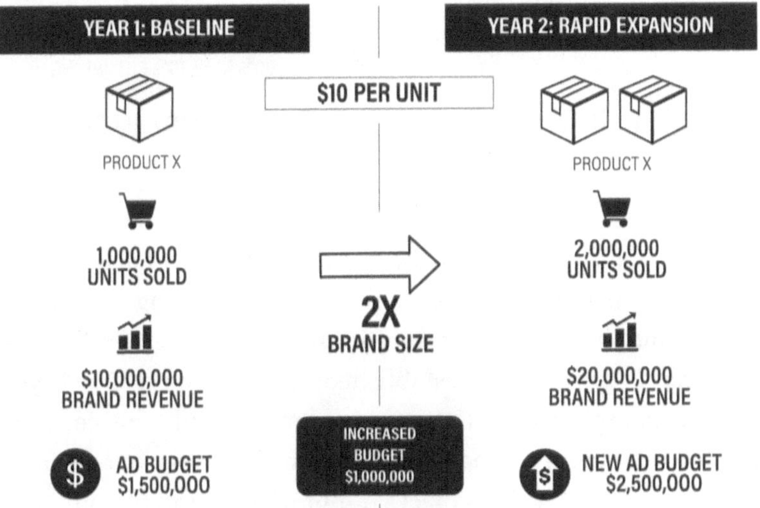

In year two, the increased year, your new budget has the ability to nearly double the size of your brand, providing great returns and rapid growth.

Now we go to the following year, year three. Let's say you hold the same budget of $2,500,000. The math needs adjusting. Here's why: First, you lost 3% due to media inflation. We will say you have a solid 10% replenishment rate. This means that 90% of the sales this year are coming from new consumers and 10% come from returning customers.

<table>
<tr><td>YEAR 2: PEAK GROWTH</td><td>YEAR 3: NEW REALITIES</td></tr>
</table>

$2.5M AD BUDGET

2,000,000
UNITS
SOLD

$20,000,000
BRAND
REVENUE

100% GROWTH

$2.5M AD BUDGET

-3%
MEDIA
INFLATION

10%
REPLENISHMENT
RATE

CUSTOMER BASE:
90% NEW/10% RETURNING

7% GROWTH

This is due to the fact that you now have to backfill non-returning customers. Now, there is nothing wrong with a 7% growth rate if you are a mature brand like Windex or Tide. In fact, that is good for an established, mature brand. But if you are an emerging brand that is competing with the category leader, it suddenly appears your brand is falling out of favor with the consumer. This places doubt in the mind of your category buyer and opens the door for your bigger competitors to chase your shelf (and your growth) space by claiming you were a fad.

Every retailer and retail buyer carrying your product is focused on one question: "What have you done for me lately?" Last year's success is nearly meaningless. They are all focused on what product mix will net them the best return and how they can increase their gross and bottom line. It is no longer good enough to just be above the minimum turn rate that the retailer expects—the brands that are above the line and showing the most upward velocity are the brands that will stay on the shelf and get additional facings. The numbers are king.

Believe it or not, we are now seeing SKUs that are doing million-dollar numbers at one account—brands that in the past would have been safe—now being delisted because their velocity is not moving upward. This is why major successful brands are constantly increasing their advertising budgets. They have learned there is no such thing as safely standing in place.

Rule 14 Questions

- What was your total ad spend last year (not counting trade spend)?
- What percentage of your sales was spent on advertising?
- What is your sales goal for the next 12 months?
- What is your replenishment rate?
- What must your budget be for the next 12 months to reach the target?

RULE 15

A GREAT BROKER WILL SAVE YOU MORE
THAN YOU WILL EVER PAY THEM

"Surround yourself with people who remind you of the future, not the past."
—Dan Sullivan

In the world of CPG, much of the business is transacted by brokers and master brokers. These are people that function as your sales staff but have long-standing relationships with the retailers.

Think of the broker as your talent agent. In the world of entertainment, agents are some of the most well-connected and powerful people in the business. For the unknown actor, they are the only road to a producer. For the producers, the agents are the gatekeepers to the biggest names.

As an unknown or less popular actor, the most important thing you can do is to get a great agent to take you on. Those talent agents are just like brokers in the CPG world; everyone wants to sign up with the best ones. In both industries, these professionals make their money on commission, so they stay away from what they don't think they can sell.

Now, we can think of retail buyers like the producers. They both know that the agent or broker knows what they are doing, they have already made millions together and they know that the agent or broker will not bring them a bad actor or, in our case, a bad product. So buyers or producers look at the agent or broker as a major part of the prescreening process.

They know that this agent or broker can spot a winner and has proven this many times in the past. This is why a great broker or agent can get a meeting with the right person in two weeks while the brand or the actor may not get a meeting in two years (or ever).

The Broker Knows

A good broker does more than get you a meeting, even though that does have tremendous value. Your broker knows the people, knows the retailer and knows what you can and cannot say no to.

Your broker will know how to build out the best presentation deck, what motivates this retail buyer, what problems this retail account may have that you can solve and, because your broker has the data, they can recommend what product to take off the shelf to fit you in.

If you are a first-time brand, the buyer is going to ask you for everything, including the kitchen sink. They will want to pay on scan (meaning you only get paid after your item crosses the scanner in store). They will want price roll backs, BOGO programs, in-store media buys, coupon buys and return discounts—the list goes on and on.

As someone new to the business (or the retailer), you will be hungry to make a deal. You will naturally really want your product on their shelf. But you do not know the retailer well enough to know what you must accept to get the deal done and what you can say no to. You need a broker.

A good broker has many products already in that store; this is why they have credibility in the first place. That experience lets them know what they (you) need to agree to and what they can push back on. And to be honest and transparent with you, some of the greatest brokers are personal friends with the people making the buying decisions, giving them far more leverage and ability to negotiate.

Typically, most brokers get five percent of actual bottom-line sales of the account they handle. In most cases, they will save you more than five percent just by knowing what to reject and getting you better terms.

But great brokers do much more than this. The really good ones spend significant amounts of money on data, oftentimes millions of dollars per year. They can provide you with insights and sales data that you cannot afford to buy when starting out. And even better, they know how to interpret the data.

Good brokers will collaborate not only with the buyer, but also the replenishment buyer. In many large accounts, the replenishment buyer is a different person than the category buyer. The category buyer decides what goes in the store. The replenishment buyer is responsible for making sure it stays available in the store and that the orders are placed at the correct timing and frequency to ensure product is available to keep shelves adequately stocked, avoiding stockouts.

A good broker will work for good product placement. This is where you appear in the planogram in store. Understandably, an eye-level position is a far more valuable position than a bottom-shelf position. The broker will also be able to negotiate temporary premium locations like endcaps.

A good broker will also make sure you are getting paid. Keep in mind that payment terms with most retailers are negotiable, and a good broker knows the best terms you can get from each retail account.

And a good broker will be there to present new items once you have your first hero product. A good broker manages the entire business to maximize profitability for everyone.

The Three Types of Brokers

There are three types of brokers in the industry: master brokers, account brokers and wannabe brokers.

Master Brokers. A master broker is essentially your vice president of sales. They typically get eight percent of net sales, and they in turn pay five percent of their fee to the account broker. A master broker makes sense for new companies with limited staff and experience since hiring a full-time person with this level of experience would be $350,000 to $500,000 annually.

Another great reason for a master broker is that he or she knows everyone in the industry. They know the retail buyers, and who the right brokers for your class of trade are at each retailer. Your master broker will be the manager of your entire broker network. They will set sales goals and hire and fire as needed to get the job done.

Brokers. Unlike a master broker, a really good broker works with limited numbers of accounts. You want brokers that have offices close to the retail accounts they call on, that are literally in the account office every week and have the ability to walk around and see people.

Some of the larger brokers today have multiple offices, such as the Barcode Group, which has offices in Bentonville (for Walmart), Minneapolis (for Target) and Seattle (for Costco). Again, you should expect to pay these brokers around five percent of net sales.

Wannabe Brokers. To be honest, of course there is not a group of brokers that call themselves wannabes, but this does not mean they do not exist. We run into these kinds of people all the time. Unfortunately, our industry does not have any licensing or governing body. So unlike a lawyer or CPA who must meet some minimum standards to practice, there is no guarantee that a broker or an advertising agency knows what they are doing. Anyone can hang out their proverbial shingle and call themselves an expert.

Sadly, for every one of us in the business that is capable and ethical, there are three more that are just charlatans either looking for their first break into the business—or worse, just trying to sell unsuspecting entrepreneurs a useless bill of goods.

The best way to find the premier brokers is personal recommendations from people within the industry. This is why I have built relationships with all the top brokers in the country—for the purpose of knowing who is good at which retailers, and to have the ability to recommend them without fear of my client getting ripped off.

Here are some things to look out for when selecting a broker:

- They tell you that they call on everyone, or claim to call on a lot of retail accounts. Unless they are a major player with a large staff and multiple offices, they are lying. Brokers generally specialize in a particular retailer or class of trade.

- They ask you for a large cash deposit or big retainer. In practice, most brokers work on flat commission. The exception to this is if you are a very new brand and need a lot of preliminary or prep work to get you ready for retail. In this case, some brokers may ask for a modest retainer that will be applied to commissions and will stop once the product goes into retail.

- The other sign of a wannabe is when you ask them what brands they currently represent and they can't (or won't) tell you. Or they may give you some line like, "We don't disclose our clients due to privacy issues." That is nonsense—do not accept that answer. By the way, you will hear that same kind of excuse from scam advertising agencies. The truth is, we are happy to brag about our past successes and who uses us.

Your broker or brokers are about to become an integral part of your organization. Not only do you need to thoroughly vet them to make sure they are capable of doing the job, but you need to have good chemistry with them, because life is a lot easier when you work with people you like and trust. This needs to be someone you want to go to dinner with and don't mind traveling with—because you will.

Rule 15 Questions

- Do you need a master broker or account brokers?
- Do you have the best broker for every account?

- Do your brokers provide data and sales figures?
- Do your brokers participate in new product development and sales projections?
- Are your brokers monitoring inventory and working to keep replenishment high?
- Do you like these people?

RULE 16

ALIGN YOURSELF WITH THE BEST "WHOS" IN THE BUSINESS

*"You don't grow by trying to do everything yourself.
You grow by finding the right 'Whos' to do the 'Hows.'"*
—Dan Sullivan

Who Not How: The Formula to Achieve Bigger Goals is a bestselling book by my friends Dan Sullivan and Dr. Benjamin Hardy. (Dan is a master of making the complicated simple.) The premise of the book comes from one of Dan's principles that he teaches at Strategic Coach®. It is simply this: When you spend all your time trying to figure out *how* to do things, your business grows very slowly, since it is now limited by your learning curve and available time. But when you identify and recruit the absolute best people (the right *"Whos"*) to do those things, your business now grows exponentially.

There are far too many specialized skills needed to build a successful CPG brand. With over 30 years in this business, and hundreds of successful products launched, I still go to the best "Whos" in the business.

For years, I was contacted by a struggling topical analgesic maker looking for solutions. Every few months, I would get a call asking me, "What should I do?" and I would tell him, but he was not yet ready to hear. Finally, on one of our calls, I broke through to him and said, "You need to advertise as I have been telling you," and "You need the right 'Whos' on your team." I explained to him that he needed to surround himself with people that are better at their job or discipline than he was.

I introduced him to an amazing master broker named David Biernbaum. Within three years, his product was in over 40,000 stores nationwide and was the number one topical pain product in all drug stores in America.

As a cautionary tale, this same company decided after this tremendous success that they no longer needed their "Whos," and today, the sales of the product are a tiny fraction of what they once were.

"Whos" come in many different forms. They are your employees, your contract manufacturers, your brokers, your advertising and marketing agency, your lawyer and your CPA.

It is important to keep in mind that you should always hire the very best you can afford and be prepared to hire "Whos" that are outside of what you can afford.

Avoid Hiring These "Whos"

Bargain "Whos": They are a bargain for a reason. Chances are they are at your level or below. You need talent that is smarter than you, and better at the "How" than you will ever be. You are not going to grow your business with the same level of thinking that got you to where you are now. The simple truth is that there is no such thing as a bargain or discount "Who"; you get "Who" you pay for.

Family or Convenient "Whos": Do not hire "Whos" based on convenience or family ties or friendship. It can be tempting to hire family, especially if you want to help them. But I cannot tell you how many clients we have had where someone's niece or nephew was made the marketing director because either it was the only spot open for them or maybe they built a website, so that made them the closest thing to an expert. My advice is to get the best "Whos" you can get, grow the company and then you can afford to pay relatives to stay home if you want to.

Big Resume "Whos": Do not hire a "Who" just because they have a major brand on their resume. Big brands have hundreds, sometimes thousands, of employees. Having the job of brand manager at The Campbell's Company, whose soup products are well-known, is vastly different than being the brand manager at a five million dollar growing brand. I have seen this scenario play out many times. The big brand manager is not used to being in the trenches and doing the actual work; they are used to having a team around them to delegate all the hard and nitty-gritty stuff to, but in a small company you need doers, not talkers.

The other problem with these big brand people is they don't know how to fight. When you are a new or emerging brand, you need to fight for every square inch of shelf space you can get. Big brands, like my example of Campbell's, are what is referred to as "category captains." They are used to having 20 to 50 items in their assortment on the shelf. When they want to roll out a new SKU, they just find a slot for the product and pull one of their own slow-sellers off. They have no idea how or what it takes to compete for three inches of shelf space. They have never had to fight for space.

Finally on this topic, when is it time to let a "Who" go and get a better "Who"? As entrepreneurs, we tend to be intensely loyal individuals. We reward loyalty by entrusting more responsibility to the people that helped us get to where we are.

There will come a time when one or more of your "Whos" will have reached their capacity to grow. Sometimes these are internal people that you have grown close to; sometimes they are even family.

Although loyalty is tremendously valuable, loyalty will not grow your business. Sometimes you have to make the hard choices and either let them go or hire someone over them. I assure you that if you are a decent human being, this will be one of the toughest parts of your job, but it is a big part of what separates the winners from the also-rans.

In Dan's words, "The right person frees up your future; the wrong person eats it." Several experts claim that investing in the right person, even one that may cost you as much as double the average salary or retainer, has a 5x to 20x impact on the business and profit over an average player. The wrong person is a 2x to 10x drain on the company.

The gap between the right and wrong person is not linear; it is exponential. The right person doesn't add to the outcome—they multiply it. They are a cultural fit and they move projects faster with fewer mistakes. The right person can add millions of dollars in value. Whether it is a broker, employee, ad agency or lawyer, the people you choose—your "Whos"—is not a place to "save" money. Making an investment in the right person can make all the difference.

Rule 16 Questions

- Are all key positions in your firm filled by the best people you can recruit?
- What is one key hire you can make this year that will change the entire company?
- Do you have the best legal and accounting team possible?
- Have you developed a relationship with a banker?

- Are you working with your advertising agency as a partner—not as a vendor?
- Does every "Who" on your team understand your goals and mission?
- Do you treat all your "Whos" like you want to be treated?

RULE 17

REAL CPG BRANDS ARE BUILT
EXPONENTIALLY, NOT INCREMENTALLY

*"We're moving from a world of scarcity to a world of abundance.
Exponential change is the new normal."*
—Peter Diamandis

For all of the online shopping we do and the increasing spend on Cyber Monday, the hard truth is that 80% of all CPG products are still sold in brick-and-mortar stores. Of that 80%, 70% is held by Walmart, Target, Costco, Walgreens, CVS and Kroger.

If you are playing in the online world only, you are unlikely to ever grow past 20% of your product's potential. Of course there are rare exceptions as in everything; for example, high-end subscription products tend to do well in the digital environment. But generally speaking, brick-and-mortar is the key to achieving your product's full sales potential.

Should You Start Small?

I often hear from clients and marketers that say, "We want to start our retail distribution slowly and grow into it." Their goal is to get into some independent or regional stores or to chase a specialty market like Sprouts Farmers Market or Whole Foods.

It is true that a regional or small store will be more likely to say "yes" to bringing in your product than a Walmart. The reason for this is quite simple: Walmart has their *Every Day Low Price* (EDLP) strategy. They can do this because they have the buying power to negotiate the lowest price with their vendors. In fact, when you become a vendor to Walmart, you will sign an agreement promising to never sell to anyone else for less.

Since smaller stores do not have price as an advantage, they need to turn the focus toward selection. This is the landscape where they can beat or compete with Walmart. Smaller stores and chains can bring in early-to-market innovative items that Walmart has not bought yet.

This strategy can be helpful, too, since some of the larger regional chains like Meijer, HEB and Publix report to *IRI* and *Nielsen*. That means that a bigger chain can look at that data and see how well you are doing at the smaller chains. This can help them make their decisions on which products to bring in or take a chance on. However, it is important to note that the advantage is also the danger.

The Small Footprint Advertising Issue

For example, let's say we have our product in Meijer, a Midwest superstore chain with 250 stores who report sales data. We must show that we can meet their minimum sales requirement (or hopefully better). If we do, great. But if we don't, we will get delisted by Meijer and subsequently will not get any other retailers to bring us in since they will know we failed at Meijer.

Now, the problem: since you are only at Meijer in this example, you cannot afford to run national TV or radio campaigns, since there are 210 TV markets in America but

Meijer is only located in less than 40 of them. Buying national TV would be extremely wasteful. Not only would you be advertising to most of the country where your product is not carried, but only 17% of Metro Detroiters shop at Meijer. (Currently 40 of the 240, or 16.5%, of Meijer Superstores are located in Metro Detroit.) So even the media running in Detroit will be losing 83% effectiveness.

You may think the answer is digital marketing; this is when the trouble starts. As a rule, digital advertising drives digital sales. If I see a product on Meta and I like it, I am just two clicks away from buying it on Amazon or even on the company's website. But digital media does a poor job of building brand awareness.

Here is a challenge for you: Quickly tell me the last digital ad you saw on your phone. Chances are you are struggling to remember one. Now, tell me one of the last TV or radio commercials you remember. I am guessing you came up with one pretty quickly.

The reason you did is because of how the human brain works. Humans think in either what is called System 1 and System 2. This model was developed by Daniel Kahneman and Amos Tversky, who received the Nobel Prize for their work. The concept was popularized in Kahneman's book, *Thinking, Fast and Slow,* and is discussed at length in my previous book, *HYPNO-TI$ING: The Secrets and Science of Ads That Sell More...*

System 1 thinking is fast, automatic and effortless. It is the snap judgment, quick reaction or impulse behavior. It is reading a billboard without thinking, knowing someone is angry or slamming on the brakes when someone cuts you off.

System 2 is slower, deliberate, effortful, logical and analytical. It is comparing one product to another, considering a purchase or doing your taxes.

Digital ads are fully in the System 1 thinking mode. They are fast and impulsive. This is why digital ads focus on having a hook in the first one to two seconds. In the digital world, if the viewer is not hooked fast, the System 1 brain skips over it.

TV and radio ads are fully System 2. They are longer, involve storytelling and give the viewer or listener an opportunity to consider the ad and be thoughtful.

Traditional media builds name recognition and brand awareness when digital does not. Digital is very impulsive and immediate action. This does not work for retail, because there is a lag time from the moment I see the message and decide I want it to the time I visit a retailer.

But remember the problem of having to show that the regional store did well or we will not stay on the shelf or get into bigger accounts. This means we must grossly overspend on advertising for the regional chain. Here is why: We have already discussed the problem with digital driving online sales as opposed to brick-and-mortar. Add on the fact that even those mostly-ineffective ads on digital are way too costly. Targeted ads on Facebook can easily cost $45 to $100 per thousand views. And this does not take into account the bots that are hitting ads with no human even seeing them.

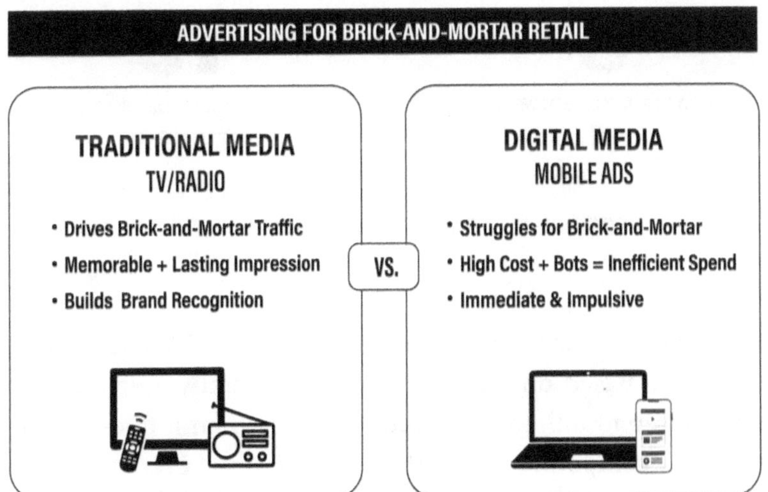

That leaves us with TV and radio. However, these are geography games; the larger the geography, the less you pay to talk to 1,000 people. As an example, let's say your customer base is a good match for *Fox News*. If you are working with an advertising agency that has great media buying skills and power like Jekyll+Hyde Labs, as of this writing you would be spending maybe $3 to talk to 1,000 viewers on a nationwide basis. But if you wanted to go buy *Fox News* in just Grand Rapids, Michigan—where Meijer is headquartered—you would have to spend between $20 on the low end and $65 on the upper end for the exact same 1,000 viewers. The same math holds true for radio.

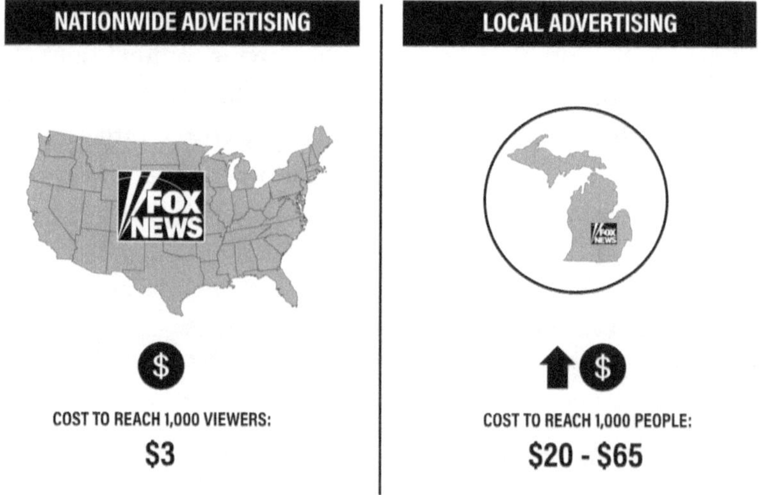

As you can see, buying local and regional TV and radio is not viable based on media efficiency. It literally costs 10 to 50 times more to talk to 1,000 people locally than it does nationally. Now compound that with the fact that not everyone shops at one chain of stores, and you can see that the media cost will kill you. We can understand that if we were in three additional chains, the advertising would be more effective both nationally and regionally because our consumer base would be expanded beyond the Meijer shopper.

What you must do is think of the first regional chain you get into as an audition. It is your chance to shine and prove you belong on-shelf. But understand; you *will* overspend on advertising, without question, if you hope to survive. To really make advertising cost-efficient, you need 70% ACV (All Commodities Volume), which means you are in 70% of viable retailers' stores. When we say 70% of all viable retailers, we mean you are in 70% of all stores that your product is appropriate for. This is why there is no slow roll. You must move as fast as possible or the cost-to-market will kill you.

The Big Chain Ride

Finally, let's talk about the reality of the sheer number of big chain stores. A "yes" from Walgreens for their full footprint is, as of this date, 8,500 stores. CVS has 9,135 stores, Walmart 4,600, Target 1,978, Kroger 2,904 and Costco 624.

If a CVS took a product in chainwide that wholesales for $10 and bought six per store, plus three per store for the warehouses, your start-up order is for 82,215 units or $822,150 on day one. Do the math on all these stores and you will see very quickly there is no crawl, then walk, then run; it is crawl, then run your ass off.

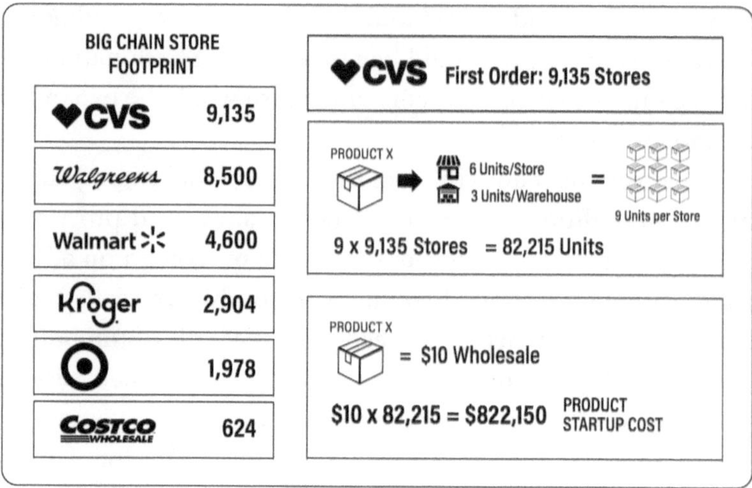

As a side note, there are many times that a major retailer will try to limit their exposure to failure and will decide to do a test of a product in just a few hundred stores. I try to resist these in most cases, but sometimes it is your only opportunity into that retailer. Some retailers like Kroger and Costco will do a test in a region which makes advertising a little easier, while others like Walmart, CVS and Walgreens will scatter the stores around the country.

Any time you are running one of these small tests, you are not trying to make any money; in fact, you will not make any money. Know that it is an audition and it will require you to overspend on advertising if you expect it to be successful to the point that you secure the balance of the chain's locations. What is important to note here is that you cannot afford to fail; you must go all in to secure the balance of the retailer's locations. If you fail the test, you will be out of that retailer with very little hope of ever getting back in again. Failure is not an option.

Once you go retail, you are all in and it can be a wild ride. You need cash on hand to build product, hold an inventory and to finance receivables which, depending on the account, can be up to 120 days. Also know that you must have inventory on hand for replenishment as these retailers will be sending you weekly replacement orders even though they have not paid for the load in order yet. If you miss delivery dates, you will get heavily fined and after three times, you will probably get delisted from the chain. They will not tolerate empty shelves.

One little piece of good news is the receivables from major chains are powerful collateral and can be financed at most banks or factors.

Rule 17 Questions

- Have you done enough research to understand the complete size of your opportunity?
- Are you trying to grow incrementally or exponentially?
- Are you building systems to grow exponentially?
- Can your supply chain withstand 10x sales growth?
- Are you prepared for short-term sacrifice for long-term success?
- Are you cash confident? Meaning, have you put yourself in a position where you do not need to drain resources from the new brand for living expenses?

RULE 18

BE WILLING TO GO WHERE YOUR COMPETITION ISN'T

Two roads diverged in a wood, and I—
I took the one less traveled by,
And that has made all the difference.

—Robert Frost

In advertising, we focus on a concept called Share of Voice (SOV). This is the math equation of how many dollars are being spent in the market to advertise a specific category of trade versus what your spend is, resulting in what your SOV is in the market. Clear as mud, right? Let's break it down.

As an example, let's assume that you are in a category where all advertisers together spend 100 million dollars annually on advertising. In order for you to have a 10% SOV, you would need the advertising spend or value of 10 million dollars.

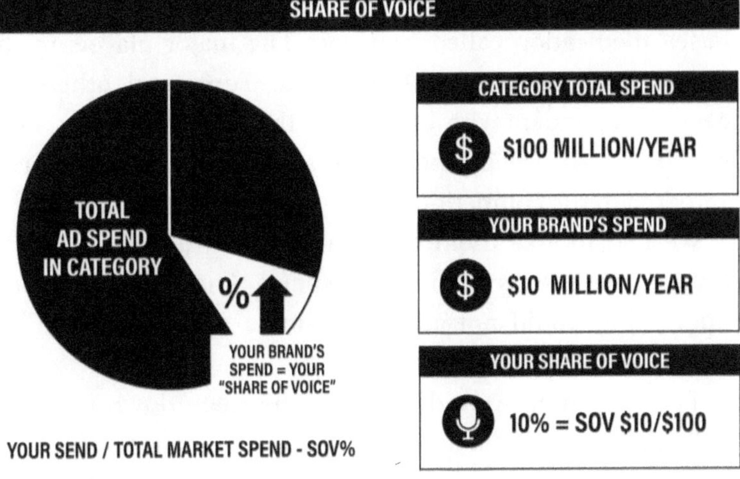

Nielsen research shows us that on average, it takes 10 points of ESOV (Excess Share of Voice) to gain one-half to one point of market share. If you are a new brand entering into a category where all advertisers together spend 100 million dollars annually on advertising, for you to gain one-half to one point of market share, you need advertising spend or value of 10 million dollars. If you are an existing brand in the category that is currently spending 10 million dollars, you need an advertising spend or value of 20 million dollars to gain an additional one-half to one point of market share.

The more money spent in your category (the more competitive), the harder this is to accomplish, while a quieter (less competitive) category would take far less money. Think of how much advertising spend goes into soda or salty snacks versus the amount of advertising spent on dental repair kits or anti-itch cream.

So if your product is in a competitive and spending category, what can you do? For emerging or ambitious brands, one of the tricks you can do is to go where everyone else is not. This allows you to stand out in that particular advertising medium.

Here's a great example: For years, we have managed a nausea medication called Nauzene. The major players in the category like Pepto Bismol, Prevacid, Tums and others are heavy TV spenders with budgets in the tens of millions each. Our client's advertising budget was frankly a rounding error compared to the competition.

We had to take them to a place where they could get an SOV and see results from the ad spend. And with the limited budget, they could not afford to run 52 weeks per year like their competitors.

The first thing we did was to niche them down to be the medicine for overindulgence. This helped narrow the category, giving them way more SOV for this particular need. Of course, Nauzene still worked for other nausea causes, but by putting the focus on a single cause, it allowed them to appear to be a leader in addressing the issue of overindulgence.

Then we created a radio campaign that ran for the week before each holiday that could lead to indulgence, starting with Thanksgiving, because who among us has not eaten too much on that day? But we also included St. Patrick's Day, Super Bowl Sunday, Memorial Day, 4th of July, Labor Day, Halloween, Christmas and New Year's Eve/Day.

We then created a comedy radio skit called *Vomit or No Vomit?* which we made sound like a really bad idea for a game show. The spot was recorded to sound like the opening to a game show with music and a big announcer's voice. The opening and closing of each spot was the same, but the middle was tailored to the specific holiday the spot was running near. This allowed for unique focused positioning around each holiday, while still giving us continuity between holidays while we were off the air.

The results were spectacular. Sales of the product significantly improved during each holiday, but more importantly, after each week, the sales went to a new average high, as we brought new consumers into our universe.

This is just one example of going where the competition is not. There are many ways to do this. You can:

- Use radio when others are not.
- Focus on TV networks that the major category spenders are not buying.
- Use print in innovative ways.
- Leverage endorsements online differently than your competitors.

This thinking can also apply to distribution. Are there retail accounts that are capable of selling your product that the category is ignoring? Can you build a case for these retailers to carry your item? Is there even a new customer market you can creatively pursue?

Rule 18 Questions

- What is your current SOV?
- How will you obtain 10 additional SOV points?
- Have you researched to find out where your competitors are advertising?
- Have you researched where they are *not* advertising?
- Have you worked with your advertising agency to discover opportunities your competition has ignored?
- What can you do differently than your competition?

RULE 19

IN-STORE MARKETING AND PRICE ROLLBACKS ARE NOT ADVERTISING CAMPAIGNS

"Competing on price is a race to the bottom. And you might win."
—Seth Godin

Buyers at chain retailers are under pressure to push their vendors to buy in-store marketing. This can include TPRs (Temporary Price Rollbacks), BOGOs (Buy One, Get One Free), in-store signage, circular promotions and even digital campaigns.

This is part of the game of retail, and you will have to say "yes" to some items. Keep in mind that different classes of trade have different demands. As an example, food and beverage will have much more pressure to spend on in-store marketing than first aid. Another thing to keep in mind is that there is a direct relationship to how much advertising you do and what your sales are, and how much in-store advertising you will have to buy from the retailer. The more money you spend in advertising, and the better your sales are, the more power you hold to say "no" to massive in-store programs.

Let's break in-store promotions into two buckets: TPRs and price offers and store-operated promotions.

TPR and BOGO. Price reductions are a good way of getting a quick boost to your POS (Point of Sale weekly sales figures) numbers if you are lagging behind and need a fast fix. However, I caution you that these price reductions can quickly turn into a drug that you can't get free of.

Doing one TPR per year to make a buyer happy and to help them reach their goals is sometimes a decision you need to make. But often we see brands with three to six rollbacks per year with the retailer. Unfortunately, this trains consumers to never buy your product at full price, since they know the product will be on sale again soon. It quickly erodes your pricing power and turns you into a discount product. Worse yet, it ruins your margins and profitability.

The truth is that in the long term, it is not a benefit to your brand. All you are doing with the rollbacks is borrowing next month's business because you conditioned people to only buy your product when it is on sale. In addition to pulling business forward, the constant conditioning of price reductions cheapens the overall brand cachet of being a premium brand.

Typically, we find that most brands running pricing rollbacks see a significant drop in sales right after the rollback. If this tactic could really build your brand, we would see a new, higher baseline of new customers coming back to replenish the product, but we rarely experience that. The following months are usually lower than the month before the rollback, showing how we simply stole sales from the future.

In-store ad programs. Every major retailer is promoting their own advertising platform. These run from website ads to magazine and circulars, in-store video or radio, floor graphics and many others. As a rule, these programs are a profit center for the retailer and are rarely a great value. (One exception is the PharmaVision program at Kroger.) Expect that you will need to participate in some fashion just to meet retailer requirements and take some pressure off of your buyer, but as is the case with rollbacks, the better your sales and stronger your advertising, the more you can say "no" to these programs.

Finally, keep in mind that in-store marketing should have a separate budget in your operating cash flow. This is not part of your advertising budget and should not be counted as advertising. It is simply a cost of doing business with a retailer.

Rule 19 Questions

- Have you created a compelling advertising campaign that will help the retail buyer feel confident in your ability to succeed?
- Have you discussed with your brokers and/or master broker what the minimum in-store programs are that you need to agree to keep each retailer?

RULE 20

AMAZON IS A RETAILER, NOT A BUSINESS

"All that glitters is not gold."
—William Shakespeare

L et me start by saying that Amazon is a great place for new and young brands to cut their teeth and learn how retail product sales work. Building a strong Amazon business is important for most CPG brands and is now the major source of product reviews. These reviews not only matter to your customers but are important for future retail chain buyers to validate that you are indeed making a quality product.

Every week, we meet marketers that have built a business on Amazon but are looking to scale beyond that. There is an easy answer to that; we covered this in Rule 17. As a reminder, 80% of all CPG products are still sold in brick-and-mortar stores, so you are only living in a 20% world if you are limited to online sales.

But the risk of being an Amazon-only seller goes far beyond the market cap that comes with digital sales. Amazon is a predatory environment. I cannot tell you how many times we have seen a successful Amazon seller have their listing shut down for no known reason and no one at Amazon is available to even discuss it. But that is just one of the risks. There are others:

Amazon the competitor: Amazon can become your competition. Once you have a product that becomes very successful on Amazon, it is not unusual for Amazon to come up with their own branded version of your item. Since they can put their item in the Amazon Buy Box and do not have an ad cost associated with the item, they can undercut you and make more money than you can.

Ad costs: Advertising on Amazon is expensive and it is a black box environment. Amazon takes a cut of your gross, charges you for shipping and then charges you for ad words to promote the product. Mysteriously, the cost frequently comes in to be just below what it is costing you to make the product.

Cheap knockoffs and Chinese counterfeits: There are many people in the Amazon space that do nothing but comb over sales figures using software programs like Helium 10 to discover what products are doing well. They then rush to China or India to make a cheap knockoff, put it on Amazon for less money, and steal your business.

Research has shown that as much as 60% of all supplements on Amazon are counterfeit products. The best case is that they have nothing harmful in them. Just make a quick visit to Alibaba.com and you will find hundreds of Chinese firms that will build whatever knockoff product you want.

These counterfeiters will put the product up on Amazon using your photos, trademarks and even your own ad copy, but they will post it at a significantly lower price. They are not only stealing your business, but they have the potential to damage your brand by being an inferior product.

Sadly, even when you chase them down through the brand registry and other legal means to stop them, they just show up a week later under another fake name and fake address. Even though this behavior puts the public in harm's way from bad products, Amazon does very little to stop it, since they make money on them just like they do on you.

Every month, we meet a company that was doing five million in sales on Amazon a year or so ago, and now, through one of these dirty tricks, they have been reduced to two million or sometimes less. It is always dangerous to put all your eggs in one basket no matter who owns the basket, but when Amazon owns it, your demise is likely not if, but when, if this is your major outlet.

Rule 20 Questions

- What percentage of your total income is
  on Amazon?
- Have you been monitoring the market for knockoffs
  or counterfeit products?
- How can you get your sales to a point where
  Amazon is 15% or less of total sales?

PART III

MINDSET

RULE 21

BUILD YOUR COMPANY TO GO BEYOND YOU

"Design your company to grow with or without you, or you'll become the bottleneck."
—Verne Harnish

You started your business with a dream: freedom, control, impact, maybe even a shot at legacy. But somewhere along the way, your business became your boss.

You wake up with a to-do list longer than your vision board. Every decision funnels through you. Every fire needs your hose. Your team doesn't move without your say-so. You're the brain, the heart and the backbone.

And you're exhausted.

You thought entrepreneurship would buy you time and wealth. But instead, you're handcuffed to a company that cannot function without you. That's not success. That's just self-employment at scale.

What's worse? You've built something that no one can buy, no one can run and no one can inherit—because you never built it to go beyond you. If you don't solve this, you'll never be free.

The Myth of Control: Why Doing Everything Feels Right—But Is Wrong

Entrepreneurs are addicts for control. We're wired that way. And early on in your business, that control is necessary. When you're just getting started, it's all on your shoulders. You have to be in the weeds.

But what makes you successful in the startup phase will kill your business in the scaling phase.

What we really need to learn is that control is an illusion. We are in control of very little, and in many cases, control is more hindrance than benefit. I will again use my love of auto racing as a metaphor to explain this.

There is a famous saying by Mario Andretti: "If everything seems under control, you're not going fast enough." What this means in racing is that to be really fast and at the top of the game, you have to allow the car to get a little out of control. If the car feels like it is running on rails, you are just not driving fast enough.

What we need to focus on in business is not control, it is influence. We need to give up this artificial grip on control and look to influence the outcome. This works in racing, business and even life in general. Control is an illusion.

At a certain point, your presence starts to become a liability. You turn into a bottleneck. You limit decisions. You slow growth. And worst of all, you make the business emotionally dependent on you.

Employees stop solving problems—they just bring them to you. Customers ask for you, not the brand. Vendors won't negotiate without your approval.

You are the linchpin, the glue...and the trap.

That's not control. That's captivity.

True freedom doesn't come from doing more. It comes from building systems, leaders and structures that can operate independently from your daily involvement.

If You Can't Sell It or Pass It On, You Built a Job— Not a Business

Let's talk brass tacks. There are only three endings for any business:

1. You sell it.
2. You pass it on.
3. It dies when you do.

If you don't build your company to operate without you, options one and two are gone. That leaves number three—and let's be honest, that's not a plan. That's a eulogy with a balance sheet.

Buyers don't want a business that needs your genius to survive. They want repeatable results, predictable systems and a team that can execute without you. That's what drives valuations. That's what gets you a check.

And if you dream of passing it to your children, don't hand them a business that breaks without Dad or Mom at the helm. They don't want to be slaves to your calendar. They want a company that works like a machine—with or without them.

Don't build a business that dies with you. Build one that multiplies without you.

Freedom Is the Goal—Structure Is the Vehicle

You didn't start this business just to create a brand—you did it to create options. You did it to create freedom. As Dan says about entrepreneurs: "We are all chasing the Four Freedoms®...":

- Freedom of Time
- Freedom Purpose
- Freedom of Money
- Freedom of Association

In other words, entrepreneurs want to do what they want, when they want, where they want and with whom they want—for what they want.

But none of that is possible without structure. Structure is what separates owners from operators. It's what gives you the leverage to step back while the business moves forward.

You need:

- Documented processes that anyone can follow
- A leadership team empowered to make decisions
- Metrics that tell the truth, even when you're not in the room
- A customer journey that doesn't require your charisma to convert
- A vision your team can own without constant micromanagement

Freedom is earned through systems. Without them, you'll always be a prisoner to your own success. But know that you don't have to build the structure and systems alone. Remember Rule 16: Align Yourself with the Best "Whos" in the Business? Find some "Whos" to help transform your vision.

Dan from Strategic Coach® has identified this as one of the items needed to scale your business faster. He calls it "Make it Up, Make it Real, Make it Recur." As the founder, you "made it up." But it will be a slow, frustrating ride if you don't find those

"Whos" to help with systems and processes as they "make it real" and "make it recur."

The Ego Addiction: Why Some Founders Can't Let Go

There's another reason founders don't scale themselves out or work themselves out of a job: ego.

We love being the hero. The smartest person in the room. The reason things work. Sometimes we set fires just so we can put them out.

But here's the truth: If your business needs you to survive, then it's not a tribute to your brilliance, it's a monument to your insecurity.

You didn't build an empire. You built a dependence.

Ego tells you that only you can do it right. That your name is the brand. That your instinct is irreplaceable. But legacy businesses aren't built on personalities, they're built on principles, products and performance.

If you want to build a company that lives beyond you, you have to kill the ego and elevate the system.

How To Architect a Business That Outlives You

Let's get tactical. Here's how you build a business that scales and sells—whether you stay or walk away.

1. Build the Machine, Not the Myth
    - Your personality doesn't scale. Systems do.
    - Create SOPs (Standard Operating Procedures) for every key function.
    - Make training replicable.
    - Remove "founder intuition" from critical decisions.

2. **Hire Leaders,** Not Helpers
    - **Stop hiring** to delegate tasks. Hire people who can own results.
    - **Empower** a COO to run daily ops.
    - **Build a leadership** team with accountability.
    - **Create ince**ntive structures that align with **company** growth.

3. Codify the Culture
    - **If your values** aren't written down, they'll **disappear** when you do.
    - **Define your** mission, vision and code of conduct.
    - **Build culture** into onboarding and **performance** reviews.
    - **Celebrate** behavior, not just results.

4. Build a Data Engine
    - **A founder**-led company runs on gut. A scalable **company** runs on metrics.
    - **Track leadi**ng indicators (not just sales).
    - **Install das**hboards that report without emotion.
    - **Use data** to make strategic decisions and drive autonomy.

5. Create Exit Options
    - **Even if** you're not ready to sell, build like you will.
    - **Clean up** your financials.
    - **Separate** founder perks from true business costs.
    - **Build an** acquisition pitch deck every year—just in case.

Your Business Should Be Generational, Not Situational

There's something noble about building for the next generation. But it doesn't happen by accident.

Too many businesses collapse because the founder never taught anyone else how to run them. Or they passed it down with no infrastructure. Or worse, the next generation just didn't want the mess.

If you want your company to be generational, it needs:

- A playbook anyone can pick up
- A vision that extends past your lifetime
- A culture rooted in process, not personality
- A structure that promotes stewardship, not dependency

Your kids should not inherit your burnout. They should inherit your blueprint.

What Happens When You Get This Right

When you build a business that doesn't need you, something amazing happens:

- You gain:
    - Time—because you're not in the weeds.
    - Options—because your company is sellable.
    - Leverage—because the machine scales faster than you ever could.
    - Peace—because you're no longer the safety net for every problem.
    - Legacy—because you built something that lasts.
- You stop:
    - Owning a job, and start owning an asset.
    - Being the engine, and start being the architect.
    - Running the business, and start leading the vision.

Final Thought: You're Either Building a Prison or a Platform

At the end of the day, you have to ask yourself one question:

Am I building something that sets me free, or something that owns me?

Too many founders spend 10, 20, even 30 years inside a business that looks like success but feels like a trap. They have cars, houses and strong revenue, but no time, no options and no exit.

Don't let that be you.

Build a business that scales. Build a business that sells. Build a business that survives you. Because if your company can't go on without you...it won't.

If this resonates with you, here's what to do right now:

1. Audit your business. What still depends on you?
2. List your exit options. Could you sell or pass it on today?
3. Find your replacement. Start grooming leaders now.
4. Document your genius. Make your playbook real.
5. Let go. Trust the systems you build.

Freedom isn't the reward for building a business. It's the requirement.

Build accordingly.

Rule 21 Questions

- Can your company run with you being gone for a month?
- Can your company grow with you being gone for a month?

- Do you have an exit plan?
- Do you want to sell the company or pass it down?
- Is a succession plan in place?
- If a sale is the goal, are you running the company to maximize the sale price?

RULE 22
ALL SUCCESS STARTS WITH THE TRUTH

"Truth is like the sun. You can shut it out for a time, but it ain't goin'
away."
—Elvis Presley

Let me give it to you straight: Every real success I have ever seen—mine or someone else's—starts with the truth. Not the spin. Not the Instagram highlight reel. The truth. And most people do not want to hear that because the truth is heavy. It makes demands. But the truth is the price of real growth. Without it, everything else is a façade.

If you are building a brand, launching a product, trying to fix your life, grow your team or break through a plateau, nothing works until you face what is real.

The Truth Doesn't Flinch—and That's Why It Works

You can have a great-looking pitch deck, sharp packaging and a killer Instagram feed, but if your product sucks, the market will punish you. If your leadership is weak, your team will disengage. If your numbers are fake, the cash flow will tell on you. Reality always collects the bill.

I can't tell you how many times I have had someone say to me that great advertising can sell anything no matter how bad the product is. No. That is simply not true. It will only work for a short time. Let me give you an example:

The movie *Joker: Folie à Deux* had a 200 million dollar production budget. The studio then spent 100 million dollars in promotion and advertising. The movie premiered in week one with a box office take of 37.8 million dollars. However, week two dropped all the way down to seven million dollars. The reason was once it was on the market, the public quickly realized it was a bad product and started telling each other and posting it on social media. Even with 100 million advertising dollars, the studio could not overcome the reality that they made a movie that superhero fans had little interest in seeing.

As a side note, the reason the movie failed is because they failed to cater to the prime superhero demographic. These are people who attend the movie to see superhuman feats and amazing special effects with stories of good overcoming evil. Instead, they created a movie with the villain as the star with no superpowers (other than insanity) and then decided that the right plan was to make it into a musical with Lady Gaga. This can be viewed as a lesson to not damage your best or hero product with another related, but subpar product. Each product must stand as a success on its own, even if it is a brand extension.

I have been in boardrooms where everyone danced around the truth until the company bled out. I have seen entrepreneurs lose millions because they wouldn't admit what the numbers were screaming. Ego kills more businesses than competition ever will.

Truth in Business: Know What You're Really Selling

Let's talk about business. If you are not clear on what your customer actually values, you are not selling—you're guessing. And guessing is gambling.

I coach companies every week and the first thing I ask is, "What problem do you solve—and how do you know?" Not, "What do you think it is?" and not, "What's your story?" I want data. I want customer feedback. I want the truth. Because once we have that, we can build something real. Something profitable. Something scalable. But not before we have the truth laid out in front of us.

Truth in Leadership: Own the Mirror

Want to lead a team? Great. Start by telling the truth about yourself:

- Where are you weak?
- What have you been avoiding?
- What decisions are you dragging your feet on because they scare you?

People follow clarity, not charisma. Your team can smell hesitation. They can see when you are ducking hard conversations or making excuses. And guess what? If you are not honest with them, they will not be honest with you. Culture starts with the leader's courage.

Truth in the Brand Game: Position or Perish

In marketing, you can either tell your story or let the market tell it for you. But here is the catch: The market only listens to what is true. You can't fake value for long. You can't gloss over weaknesses forever. So if your product has a flaw—fix it. If your price is off—test it. If your offer does not convert—rewrite it.

A winning brand doesn't come from pretending. It comes from precision. A winning brand comes from doing everything right and doing the right thing no matter how difficult it is. It comes from following all 27 unbreakable rules, being painfully honest with yourself and your team, surrounding yourself with the best people and never, ever, ever giving up.

Picture one of these big modern slot machines you see at casinos. Now imagine it has 30 different boxes or windows on the screen. Your job is to get as many of these boxes to display "winner" as possible. The fewer boxes you get right, the lower your odds of success.

Why Most People Run From the Truth

People run from the truth because it's hard. That's it. The truth forces you to change. It forces you to fire someone or pivot or spend money for which you didn't plan. It forces you to kill your darlings—the features no one uses, the campaigns that don't convert, the stories that don't resonate. It means letting go of comfort.

But here is the paradox: Every breakthrough lives on the other side of that discomfort. Want bigger revenue? Better health? Category authority? Start telling the truth about where you actually are and what is not working. The biggest human fear is the fear of change, yet change is the only way to make our lives, businesses and world better.

In Sales, Marketing, Life—Truth Is the Lever

When I teach messaging, I don't start with copywriting tricks. I start with the truth. What is the core pain your customer has?

What is the real transformation you deliver? Get that right and you don't need to sell—you just need to show up. Selling is always focused on getting someone to buy what you are selling. When you are telling the truth and you have created a product that enhances the user's life, you have transcended selling and moved to educating.

Great offers don't sell because they are clever. They sell because they are honest. Honest about the problem. Honest about the solution. Honest about the stakes.

The same goes for your personal brand. Don't build a persona. Build a platform based on values you actually live. That is the only kind of brand that lasts. Just like a politician or a celebrity has a platform to espouse their values, your brand is a platform. It should be a reflection of who you are and what you stand for, and it should always be easy to see what your floor is—that which you will not go below.

You Cannot Fix What You Won't Face

Here is a principle I live by: "You can't solve a problem you're still lying about."

Your P+L doesn't lie. Your cholesterol numbers don't lie. Your spouse doesn't lie (if you're actually listening). Most of the time, the truth is already on the table. You just have to stop pretending it's not there.

How To Get Real: Start Here

Do you want to align with truth and build something that lasts? Here is your checklist:

1. Track the Data
2. Audit Your Life and Business
3. Surround Yourself with Truth-Tellers

4. Say the Hard Thing First
5. Let Go of What No Longer Works

Truth Isn't a One-Time Fix—It's a Discipline

You don't arrive at truth. You live it every day, in every decision. You get honest about where your business is. You face the flaws in your model. You speak truth in meetings. You tell yourself the truth about your own energy, your habits and your attitude.

Success is not complicated; it's just expensive. And the down payment is always truth.

Final Word: Stop Polishing Lies and Start Building Something Real

There is a lot of noise out there. Gurus. Funnels. Hacks. Trends. You can spend a lifetime polishing your image and never build anything that matters.

Or...you can tell the truth.

Once you tell the truth, everything changes. Alignment kicks in. Strategy sharpens. Teams move faster. Brands connect. Money shows up. Because truth is magnetic. And success doesn't just like truth—it demands it.

Rule 22 Questions

- Are you being honest with yourself about your business?
- What are the customer problems you really solve?
- What is your real brand story?
- What is your real mission?
- What have you been avoiding that needs to happen now?

- What lies are you telling yourself that are hurting your business?
- Are you managing by the numbers?
- Have you surrounded yourself with "yes" men or truth-tellers?
- Are you willing to kill off anything that is not serving you?

RULE 23

BE WILLING TO PROVE YOU DESERVE A SEAT
AT THE BIG TABLE

"If they don't give you a seat at the table, bring a folding chair."
—Shirley Chisholm

L et me make this clear right up front: Nobody owes you a seat at the table—not in consumer products, not in business and not in life. If you want to play in the big leagues, you better be willing to prove you belong there. Over and over again. That is the cost of admission.

Many times, I've sat across the table from people who thought having a decent product was enough. They would slap a label on a bottle, spin up a Shopify site and wonder why Walmart wasn't calling. The truth? They hadn't done the work. They weren't ready. And the market doesn't reward good intentions; it rewards execution.

You need to make it obvious for consumers why you exist, what the lane is that you run in and how you own your lane.

If you want to get into the big world of consumer products —retail, DRTV (Direct Response Television), e-commerce, wholesale and QVC—you must show up with more than passion. You need positioning, proof, professionalism and a relentless willingness to evolve. This is war, and every inch is earned. Start with the brutal truth.

If your product is not selling, you do not have a business; you have a hobby. And if you cannot scale, you are not in the big world yet; you're just in orbit. The people who succeed in this space don't just build products; they build systems, pipelines, partnerships and brands that can handle pressure. And none of that happens by accident.

What Do Winners Do?

What separates winners from the rest? Winners don't just want it; they prove it. They prove it by knowing their customer better than the competition. They prove it by testing every assumption. They prove it by staying in the game long enough to be taken seriously. And more importantly, they know when to adapt.

Let me tell you something most people won't say out loud: The market doesn't care how hard you work. It doesn't care about your origin story. The buyer at Target or Walgreens is looking at one thing: Can you move product? To do so initially and continuously, you also have to answer these questions:

- Do you know your numbers?
- Can you support a campaign?
- Will your supply chain hold?

Do you want to be in that room? Prove it. Show the buyer that they did not make a mistake meeting with you. Show them that you belong in the meeting room with them. Do everything possible to make it easy for them to say "yes."

Do not just bring them an idea; bring a movement. Bring data. Bring conversion rates, reorder velocity, demo footage and influencer partnerships. Bring proof that your product doesn't just exist—it wins.

I have worked with brands that have gone from basement-bottling operations to shelf space in national chains. And not one of them got there by hoping. They got there by treating their product like a company from day one.

They invested in messaging before margins. Real winning companies will cut their own pay before they cut the ad budget. They learned to tell the story before asking for the sale. They didn't cry about copycats—they focused on being the best. They didn't ask for permission. They asked for results.

If you are not willing to prove you belong in the big leagues, let me save you the trouble: Stay out. It will eat you alive.

Because this world isn't just competitive; it's brutal. You are up against billion-dollar companies with bottomless ad budgets and supply chains built like Swiss watches. They don't sleep. And they don't lose often.

So what do you do? You outthink them. You outmaneuver them. You outprove them. You build a better offer. You go niche before you go national. You overdeliver until you become undeniable. As Joe Polish says, "Your offer is always bigger than your ask."

You do not just say, "My product is great." You *demonstrate* that it converts, that it retains customers, that it generates reviews organically and that influencers want to be associated with it.

Proving you belong in this game means doing the boring stuff right. Over and over. Supply chain. Compliance. Labeling. Claims substantiation. Payment terms. Inventory flow. That's what real players focus on.

Anybody can come up with an idea. Winners are the ones who follow through.

Now let me talk directly to the entrepreneur who wants to be in Walmart or Costco or Kroger or Vitamin Shoppe. Don't show up with hope; show up with answers. Be prepared with backup.

You need to show them your:

- Unit economics
- Support strategy
- Commitment to velocity, not just volume
- Contingency plans

Because they don't want to babysit you; they want a partner.

I have helped hundreds of products cross that invisible line from startup to enterprise. Every one of those entrepreneurs and top leaders had one thing in common: They were willing to put their ego aside and prove they deserved to be there.

That means refining your brand, evolving your packaging, testing dozens of price points, split testing landing pages and walking away from features you loved that didn't convert.

It means listening to hard feedback. And making changes. Fast.

It means hiring better people than you. And trusting them.

It means obsessing over your customers until you know their pain better than they do.

Do you want to be in the big world? Start acting like you already are.

- Stop waiting for permission.
- Stop copying competitors.
- Stop trying to be everything to everyone.
- Build something specific.
- Build it on truth.
- Build it to last.

I will say it again: The market doesn't care what you want. It cares about what you can *prove*.

And if you can prove that your product works, that your customers love it and that your infrastructure can support demand, then, and only then, the big world will pay attention.

But here is the secret: By the time they notice, you won't be asking for a seat at their table. You'll be too busy building your own.

Rule 23 Questions

- Do you have a hobby or a business?
- Are you 100 percent all in on your brand?
- How willing are you to take "no" as an answer?
- Can you back up every promise you make or are you just spitballing?
- Are you prepared to show how you will drive traffic to retailers' shelves?
- Have you surveyed your current customers for honest feedback?
- Have you studied your own cognitive biases and learned to set them aside? (If you want to learn more about the biases we all have and the psychology of selling, read my book *HYPNO-TI$ING: The Secrets and Science of Ads That Sell More.*)
- Do you have the mindset of getting up more times than you get knocked down?

RULE 24

NEVER BELIEVE THAT YOU HAVE ALL THE ANSWERS

"Success is a lousy teacher. It seduces smart people into thinking they can't lose."
—Bill Gates

For those of you reading that are entrepreneurs like me, you have a strength that is also a weakness. When you started out, all you had was an idea of what could be. The people around you, even some people who were very close to you, probably told you that you were making a bad choice to give up a steady job and set out on your own. And what happened? You proved them all wrong.

Being an entrepreneur is not a career choice. Entrepreneurs are not made; they are born this way. My friend Dr. Doug Brackmann's book *Driven* can provide you with a great understanding of the entrepreneurial brain. Dr. Brackmann demonstrates that entrepreneurs make up around four to five percent of the population, and that it is based on gene expression.

Those with these specific gene expressions are driven to success and are not afraid of risk. I am one of these people. Most of us that are hardwired like this knew we were different by the time we were around five to eight years old. In the book, he shows how these personalities gravitate towards entrepreneurship, as well as being professional athletes, inventors, adventurers and Navy SEALS. It is worth the effort to know if this is you.

Another great book on this, from Gino Wickman, is called *Entrepreneurial Leap*. In his book, Gino lays out the true attributes of an entrepreneur and gives the reader the tools to self-assess.

As an entrepreneur, this is your life. You keep proving the "Negative Nancys" in your sphere wrong over and over again, which is awesome, but now comes the other side of the coin. It's called human conditioning. Our unconscious minds are pattern-recognition machines. This is why, when you get into your car in the morning, you do not have to figure out how to start it or what a steering wheel does. It is programmed into you due to repetition, which is obviously useful and necessary to function even somewhat efficiently in life.

Unfortunately, this pattern recognition system also seduces you into thinking that only you have the right answers. After all, your mind reasons, *every time someone told me I was wrong, I was right!* The problem is all those "Negative Nancys" in your life are not experts in the CPG world—they are just people with opinions. Many of those opinions are not the least bit helpful to you, so you dismiss them—as you should. However, you must break this pattern, surround yourself with people that know more than you and be willing to listen.

The moment you think you've got all the answers in consumer-packaged goods, you're already losing. In fact, if you're not constantly learning, testing, adjusting and challenging your own assumptions—get out now. The CPG game isn't for the complacent. It's for the obsessed.

Know this: CPG doesn't reward arrogance. It punishes it. Hard.

I have been in the industry long enough to know that the biggest killer of great products is not the competition—it is ego. I have watched brands flame out, not because their packaging sucked or their margins were off, but because the founder stopped listening. They thought they knew it all. And when the market shifted, they didn't.

Here's the truth most people can't swallow: The market doesn't care what you believe—it cares what you can prove. And just when you think you've nailed your customer, your category or your channel—that's when something changes. Trends evolve. Retail resets. Cost of goods shifts. The algorithm moves. And now you're playing defense instead of scaling.

Success in CPG is not about being right at one or two moments. It is about staying responsive. That means you never assume your last win will buy your next one. You never assume that what worked in DTC will work in retail. And you definitely never assume that your gut is more reliable than data. It's not.

CPG Is a Game of Humility

Every brand you admire—from KIND to RXBAR to Oatly—had to pivot. Multiple times. Not because they were wrong, but because they were learning. That's the game. If you're not willing to do that, you're building a monument to your ego—not a company that wins.

I have seen entrepreneurs fall in love with their label design and ignore customer confusion. I have seen founders double down on a flavor no one is buying because "they" like it. That's not business; that's denial and ego.

Do you want to win in CPG? You better be willing to kill your darlings. You better be willing to throw out your favorite tagline because it's not converting. You better be willing to relabel, reformulate, reprice—and do it all again next quarter.

The best in this business are humble enough to test and smart enough to let go and make the needed changes.

Data Over Ego—Every Time

Do you want to grow a real brand? Then your opinion is just a starting point. Data is your decision-maker. You need to test and evaluate the data.

Test your price points. Test your offer stack. Test your demo script. Test your packaging hierarchy. Remember that you're not in the "great ideas" business, you're in the "validated performance" business. Until you prove it works at scale, it is just theory.

Do not fall in love with your assumptions. Fall in love with iteration.

Let me tell you something you must do: You must listen. The customer will tell you everything you need to know if you are willing to listen. Listen to your reviews. Your returns. Your reorder rate. Your cart abandonment rate. All of it is feedback. And feedback is not failure—it is data. It is a map.

But too many founders ignore the feedback. In a sense, they ignore the truth they don't want to hear. So they brush off the data. They write it off. They tell themselves stories like, "That customer just didn't get it." Or worse, "We're not for everyone."

That might be true, but if you are not for anyone, you've got a problem.

Retail Will Humble You Fast

Do you think you are ready for Target or Kroger? Think again. Retail is a beast, and it eats arrogance for breakfast. You walk in thinking you've got the best thing since sliced bread, and the buyer hits you with questions like, "What's your velocity in this channel?" or "What's your trade spend strategy?"

And you freeze.

Because you never thought past your product and the logo on the shelf.

Retail success is not about getting listed. That's just one hurdle. Retail success is about getting *reordered*. That means you better know your pull strategy. You better have your field teams ready. You better be sampling, demoing, geo-targeting and retargeting.

Or you are just shelf décor.

The brands that survive retail are the ones that treat every store like a new test, every region like a fresh launch and every customer as if they are the only one that matters.

Successful brands don't assume they have arrived. They assume they're always earning it.

Channels Change. Stay Nimble.

Maybe you were crushing it online during COVID. Great. But that wave ended. If you didn't diversify into retail, subscription or partnerships, you're probably feeling it.

Maybe you dominated a niche audience on Facebook ads. Perfect. But what happens when your Customer Acquisition Cost (CAC) triples and your Lifetime Customer Value (LCV) flattens?

If you assumed the channel was the business, you're toast.

Smart brands don't anchor themselves to one strategy. They stay nimble. They move where the market moves. They build omnichannel presence. They invest in what is working and cut what's not.

And they do it quickly—without ego, without drama and without emotional attachment.

Your Team Needs You To Be Curious

If you are the founder, the CEO or the visionary, you set the tone. And if you act like you have all the answers, your team stops thinking. They stop innovating. They stop challenging you.

And that's how you go from momentum to mediocrity.

Your job is not to be the smartest person in the room. Your job is to build a room full of people who are smarter than you in key areas—formulation, compliance, logistics, finance and creative. And then? Listen to them.

Ask better questions. Reward people who challenge the status quo. Make it safe to say, "We were wrong."

Because in CPG, the goal is not perfection. The goal is performance.

Innovation Comes From Uncertainty

The magic happens when you admit what you don't know.

You try a weird partnership. You explore a new ingredient. You test a risky headline. You launch a limited-run SKU. Not because you *know* it will work—but because you are willing to find out.

That is where the winners live: in the discomfort. In the questions. In the data. In the field.

The losers? They hide in certainty. They hide in false safety and protection. They keep doing what is comfortable until the business runs dry.

You don't build the next category king by being safe. You build it by being smart, fast and fearless. And none of that starts until you see the truth, drop the act and get real.

Final Word: Stay Teachable or Stay Stuck

The biggest compliment I can give a founder is this: They're teachable. Not trendy. Not loud. Not brilliant.

Teachable.

Because that's what this business demands.

Do you want to scale? Stay curious. You want to grow? Stay humble. You want to win? Stay willing to be wrong. And embrace the truth.

In CPG, success doesn't belong to the one who knows the most. It belongs to the one who learns the fastest.

So never believe you have arrived. Never assume you have mastered it. And never, ever believe you have all the answers.

Because the second you do, the game moves without you.

Rule 24 Questions

- Are you a hardwired entrepreneur?
- Is your product about building a great company or stroking your ego?
- Are you willing to kill all your darlings?
- Are you constantly testing everything?
- Are you capable of pivoting when needed?
- Have you surrounded yourself with people that possess the traits you do not have?
- Are you teachable?

RULE 25

THE BEST WAY TO PREDICT THE FUTURE IS TO CREATE IT

"Had I asked people what they wanted, they would have said: faster horses."
—Henry Ford

I came up with Rule 25 about 15 years ago in a book I wrote called *Future You: How to Predict, Design, and Live the Future You Want Now.*

Everyone wants to know: What is the future of CPG? What trends, what platforms, what ingredients are next?

You know what? Forget the crystal ball. The best way to predict the future is to *create* it.

Let me be blunt. In consumer-packaged goods, no one is handing out the road map to success. While this very book can provide great benefit to you, it's not a playbook—it's the rule-book. Just like the classic book *According to Hoyle* by Richard L. Frey tells you what the rules are for various skill and chance games, and gives some basic advice, but doesn't provide the full strategy. That part is up to you. It's the same in the CPG world. There is no master plan, no safe path. If you are waiting for the industry to hand you the playbook, you are already behind.

The winners in this game don't follow. They don't wait. They lead. They build. They invent the game other people want to play.

You don't create the future by hoping. You create it by executing relentlessly. By identifying a need before it is mainstream. By solving a pain point the consumer does not even fully understand yet. You do it by listening harder, moving faster, testing smarter and never assuming yesterday's wins will get you through tomorrow.

That is what separates product people from brand builders. Anyone can slap a logo on a label. But creating the future? That takes vision. It takes guts. It takes the kind of obsession with excellence that keeps you up at night because you know you're onto something real.

Take a look at any brand that changed the game. RXBAR didn't wait for permission to redefine clean-label snacks. They stripped it down, sold it with transparency and took over a shelf nobody was even thinking about. Liquid I.V. saw the hydration game before the rest of the industry woke up. Olipop leaned into the idea that soda could actually be functional and good for you. These brands didn't guess the future—they built it.

First, creating the future in CPG starts with clarity of mission. If you don't know exactly who you're serving, why you're serving them and how your product fits into their life, you're building blind. So first, you need to know your customer better than they know themselves. You need to understand their lifestyle, their fears and their aspirations. You create the product that solves the problem they haven't even articulated yet.

When we helped launch WaxRx, the buyers at major retailers thought we were crazy and said "no" to the product. They felt that no one was going to pay $40 to remove earwax when every other product on the shelf was $8.99. Using their conventional wisdom, they "knew" that we had gone far beyond what price elasticity would allow.

However the team at Jekyll+Hyde Labs and our client knew we were not competing with $9 eardrops; we knew we were competing with a trip to the doctor's office to have earwax removed that the $9 drops could not resolve. We did not focus on the price gap between $8.99 and $40. We focused on the convenience gap between taking hours out of your day to sit in a doctor's office and being able to fix your problem in a few minutes at home. We are not selling ear drops; we're helping people buy their time back. As they say, the rest is history—and WaxRx is now the number-one-selling earwax removal kit in the nation.

Second, you need to move fast. If you are in love with perfection, you will die in development. Get your MVP (Minimum Viable Product) out, test it, get real feedback and refine. Speed is your best friend. The consumer's attention span is short, and the shelf is crowded. You don't have time for hesitation. You need a culture of urgency.

Third, invest in your brand like it is your moat, because it is. Your brand, like a moat, is what protects your castle from outside attackers. Packaging is your first handshake. Messaging is your voice. The way you position your product will define how the market sees you and whether you stand out or disappear. Let me tell you, mediocrity is invisible. You need to be bold. You need to plant a flag in the ground that says, "This is who we are. This is why we exist." And you had better believe it.

You also need to build infrastructure like you are already national, even if you're just getting started. Logistics, supply chain, compliance—none of that is sexy, but it's what separates dreamers from operators. Retail doesn't reward good ideas. It rewards execution. Do you think Walmart wants to hear your story? No. They want to know if you can keep the shelf full, deliver on time and hit the velocity.

This is not the place for wishful thinking. This is where the grown-ups play.

Creating the future does not mean doing it alone. It means surrounding yourself with people smarter than you. People who see around corners. Experts in advertising, law, accounting, Amazon strategy, design, regulatory, finance and revenue. Your ego doesn't scale—your team does.

Let's talk about innovation. Everyone throws that word around, but most people don't understand what it really means. Innovation is not just about ingredients or formats. It's about how you solve problems. It's about experience. It's about how you make the customer feel. Maybe your product isn't new, but your delivery model is. Maybe your formulation isn't patented, but your message is crystal clear and emotionally magnetic.

Innovation also means staying uncomfortable. Anyone that has listened to me on podcasts has heard me say one of the great problems in America right now is the aggressive pursuit of comfort. As a hobby, I am a race car driver. In order to get good at it, I have had to force myself into being comfortable being uncomfortable. I must push the car and myself to new limits, where from time to time, things will go very wrong. As Andretti said: "If you are not a little out of control, you are not trying hard enough." This statement is just as true in business and in life.

The brands that last are the ones that constantly iterate. They stay paranoid. They are willing to be uncomfortable. They study their metrics. They ask questions nobody else is asking. If your brand is static, it's dying. If your team isn't stretching, they're settling.

Here is what I know from years in this industry: Your speed of execution is more important than your idea. Your resilience is more important than your branding. Your ability to adjust on the fly is more important than your initial strategy. So stop asking, "What's going to happen?" Start asking, "What are we going to make happen?"

This is where the future is built—in the trenches. It is built during the late nights, the hard pivots and the uncomfortable meetings. The founders who win are the ones who fall in love with the process. They don't fear the unknown—they build into it.

Look, there is no blueprint. But there are patterns. And the pattern is this: The bold ones win. The ones who test aggressively, who listen obsessively, who never stop evolving. That is who owns tomorrow.

Do you want to be that brand that disrupts a category? Then stop trying to follow someone else's path. Start blazing your own. Stop reading tea leaves and start building something undeniable.

Because in CPG, success does not go to the most funded. It goes to the most focused. The ones who decide they are not going to chase trends—they are going to define them.

Let me leave you with this: If you want to predict the future of your brand, stop obsessing over what competitors are doing and start obsessing over how to make your customer's life better. Period.

You create the future by delivering insane value, obsessing over execution and being relentless in your belief that the world needs what you're building.

So forget predictions. Get to work.

Because the future is waiting for you to create it.

Rule 25 Questions

- Are you using hope as a strategy?
- Is your mission clear, concise and understood by all?

- Do you know with who or what you are really competing?
- Are you really investing back in your brand?
- Are you staying uncomfortable?
- Are you constantly improving?
- Are you focused?
- Do you have a clear vision for the future with timetables and deliverables?
- Are you constantly developing future plans to stay ahead of the market?

RULE 26

ALWAYS BE THE BEST IN CLASS AND BE WILLING TO TAKE RISKS

"Are you playing to win or playing not to lose?"
—Mark Young

I often meet entrepreneurs or even existing brand operators that are playing not to lose instead of playing to win. Playing not to lose is fighting to hold on to the status quo. It is the baseball player that wants to steal second base while keeping their foot firmly placed on first. Our own cognitive biases can suck us into this thinking. It happens to all of us, including me.

In 2023, I was taking a run at a Guiness World Record in auto racing. The goal was to become the oldest professional rookie driver in history. In order to do this, I had to make the jump into a pro racing series and complete the race.

As the team and I prepared for this, it became obvious to me that I was playing not to lose. I was focused on getting to the end of the race without crashing out and lost focus on the fact that auto racing is about coming in first. (Or as race car driver Ricky Bobby famously says in the movie *Talladega Nights: The Ballad of Ricky Bobby*: "If you ain't first, you're last.")

I had to shift my thinking to entering a race for the purpose of winning, not just driving around the track. I had to go in with the intention of earning a win, not just participating. I am happy to report that not only did I complete the race and get the Guiness record, but I also placed first in that race.

If you are not playing to be best-in-class, what are you even doing in the CPG industry? This is not a space for "good enough." It is not a place for the second-tier, half-committed or overly cautious. In CPG, you either lead your category or you disappear into the noise. And if you're not willing to take risks, then don't be surprised when your brand fades into the background.

Here is the truth: Nobody remembers the "safe" brands. Consumers don't fall in love with average. Retailers don't give premium shelf space to the bland. And investors don't bet on companies playing it small. The only brands that win are the ones that go all in on quality, on identity and on risk.

Best in class is not a title you declare. It is a standard you live. Every SKU, every label, every unboxing moment needs to scream, *this brand knows who it is, what it stands for and why it matters.* From your formulation to your fulfillment, from your social content to your shelf placement, everything is either rein-forcing your greatness or eroding it.

Being best in class means you obsess over execution. You care about taste, texture, tone and timing. You don't just meet expectations, you reset them. You become the brand that competitors study and copy because you've stopped trying to be like anyone else.

But let's get one thing straight: You cannot be best in class if you're scared to take risks.

Risk is the price of entry for innovation. The entire CPG landscape shifts every 18 months. There are new platforms, new retailer partnerships or ownership, new regulations and new behaviors. If you are waiting for certainty, you'll never make a move. The brands that thrive are the ones that embrace speed, test relentlessly and pivot with purpose.

Let me break this down into two parts: (1) what it really means to be best in class, and (2) how to take strategic risks without losing your shirt.

Part 1: Best in Class Is Earned, Not Claimed

Being best in class starts with clarity. You need to know exactly who your customer is and what problem you are solving for them. There can be no fluff or founder bias—just raw, validated insight. If you can't say in one sentence what transformation your product delivers, you're not ready.

Best-in-class brands are ruthless about experience. Every detail matters. Packaging isn't just a container; it's a billboard. Flavor isn't just functional; it's emotional. Messaging isn't just informative; it's identity. If any piece of your brand feels like an afterthought, you're already losing ground. Fix it.

You can't outsource excellence. You need a pulse on every part of your business, from how your box opens to how your follow-up email reads. Don't settle for "pretty good." Your customer won't.

True excellence means knowing your numbers cold—gross margin, COGS, contribution margin, return rate and churn rate. These aren't accounting metrics. These are performance indicators. They tell the story of how well your product is actually doing.

Excellence also means relentless storytelling. Best in class brands don't just sell, they build belief. They make the customer feel like they are part of something bigger. Whether it is health, performance, sustainability or personal empowerment, great brands stand for something that matters.

Part 2: Risk Is the Multiplier for Greatness

Now, let's talk about risk.

Too many CPG founders play small because they are scared. Scared of launching too soon. Scared of trying a bold message. Scared of a new channel, new price point or new strategy. That fear is the death of momentum. They are not playing to win; they are playing not to lose, which means they already lost. Playing not to lose is a losing strategy.

Let me say it plainly: Comfort doesn't scale.

If you want to grow, you need to push the limits. You test new formats. You take a shot on retail even if it is not perfect. You bet on a bolder campaign. You build in public and learn in real time.

Risk is not recklessness; it's calculated conviction. It's knowing the downside, preparing for it and then making the leap anyway. Smart risk is how you break through the noise.

Remember: Every CPG brand you admire today took risks. They launched when it wasn't ready. They priced higher than the category norm. They told a story no one else was telling. And that is why they made it.

The Intersection of Excellence and Risk

The magic happens when best in class meets bold action.

You create products that feel like premium experiences—and then you market them like you mean it. You partner with creators, not influencers. You design packaging that turns heads and sparks curiosity. You don't wait for permission. You lead the customer to the future they didn't know they wanted.

Steve Jobs was told no one wanted a tiny player that held 1,000 songs; in fact, the tech existed and failed. But of course we know Jobs went on to invent the iPod and Apple Music.

They also told him no one wanted a cell phone that looked

like a tiny computer screen. Jobs went on to invent the iPhone and many other breakthrough products while Nokia believed in their technology and rolled out SMS text messages despite everyone thinking it was a dumb idea.

Imagine the response when they decided to let people type messages to each other on tiny keys and screens instead of just hitting speed dial. All of these were game changers with new rules and standards.

You don't build a great brand by playing by someone else's rules. You build them by setting your own standards—and then executing them better than anyone else.

This means hiring before you are ready. Launching before you are comfortable. Making offers before you feel "qualified." That's the game.

And here's the kicker: The more you commit to being best in class, the more risk you'll have to take because standing out is inherently uncomfortable. You will attract criticism. You will get copied. You will have deals fall through. But if you play not to lose—if you stay average—you will lose by default.

Don't Just Play To Win—Play To Dominate

CPG is not for the passive. This industry rewards the relentless.

Do you want to be best in class? Then act like it. Build systems that scale. Measure everything. Train your salespeople. Rehearse your pitch. Document your SOPs. Obsess over your trial-to-repeat ratio. These are the basics—and too many founders skip them.

Excellence is not accidental. It is built on discipline. Discipline sounds like something to avoid, but true self-discipline is the key to success and freedom.

And risk? It's your accelerant. The right risks shorten the timeline. They draw attention. They create movement in the market. When you combine high standards with high courage, you become unstoppable.

The most valuable brands in CPG didn't get there because they were safe. They got there because they made bold bets. Bets on themselves, on their customers and on their team.

So here is the real challenge: How high are you willing to set the bar, and how far are you willing to go to reach it? Are you willing to delay the easy sale for the right partner? Are you willing to cut a hero SKU because the data says it is underperforming? Are you willing to risk embarrassment to try something new?

That is the difference between good and great. Between the ones who dabble and the ones who dominate. You don't build legacy brands by standing still. You build them by moving fast, staying sharp and never accepting "good enough." You paint the airplane in the air.

This industry is brutal—but it's also wide open. There's space at the top for the ones who are ready to claim it.

So don't just be good. Be unforgettable.

And don't just take risks. Take the right ones—at the right time—with everything you've got.

That is how you become best in class. And that's how you stay there.

Rule 26 Questions

- Is your product really the best in class?
- Are you working to make your product better?
- Are you close to the highest price in class?
- Are you constantly perfecting your customers' experience with you?
- Do you know all your numbers by heart?

- Have you crafted a story that allows customers and staff to be a part of something bigger?
- Are you ready and willing to take big, calculated risks?
- Are you running your brand to win or to just not lose?
- Are you willing to cut dead items from your product line?
- Are you playing not to lose or playing to win?
- Are you willing to make short-term sacrifices to get the long-term reward?

RULE 27

NEVER BE PARTIALLY PREGNANT; BE ALL IN

"Commitment is what transforms a promise into reality."
—Abraham Lincoln

Let's get something straight right out of the gate: You cannot be partially pregnant. You either are or you are not. And the same brutal truth applies to the consumer-packaged goods business; you are either all in or you're already dead and don't know it yet.

This business is not for the faint of heart. It isn't for tourists. It isn't for dabblers, dreamers or dilettantes. CPG is a full-contact sport. If you do not have the stomach to bleed a little, hustle hard and make some enemies along the way, then do yourself a favor and walk away now. This isn't a weekend side hustle. It's war.

The Myth of the Safe Launch

Every week, I see founders trying to hedge their bets. They launch a product with one toe in the water and a backup plan in their back pocket. They throw up a Shopify site, spend $500 on Meta ads, ship a few dozen units to a boutique store and call it "launching a brand."

Let me be clear: That's not launching a brand—that's playing dress-up.

If you think you can tiptoe into this space and see if it "catches on," you are already behind. This industry eats the hesitant alive. The people who win in CPG are the ones who go all in financially, emotionally and operationally. They don't ask, "What's the minimum I can do?" They ask, "What's everything I need to do, and how fast can I start?"

The Commitment Test: Burn the Boats

If you are standing on the shore, looking at the sea of competition in this industry, let me tell you what the winners do: They burn the boats.

There is no plan B. No fallback. No "I'll try this for six months and if it doesn't work, I'll go back to corporate." No. That is not how this works. When you are all in, you make different decisions. You fight harder. You push past limits you didn't know you had. And guess what? The market notices.

Retail buyers can smell half-heartedness from a mile away. They see it in your packaging, your sell sheet, your trade show booth, your pricing strategy and your social presence. If you are not all in, they know it—and they will pass on you and your product. Because if you don't believe in your product with full conviction, why the hell should they?

What All In Actually Looks Like

So what does being all in actually look like? It is not about spending recklessly or quitting your job prematurely. It is about mindset, strategy and commitment. Here is what I mean:

1. You Build a Moat Before You Build a Logo

Forget the branding agency and the fancy labels—at least at first. What matters is the product and the positioning. Can you tell me, in 10 seconds, why your product is a no-brainer for your target consumer? Can you explain how it is different, better or cheaper than what is already on the shelf?

If you cannot, you are not ready. Because when you're all in, you build your business on customer insight, not Canva templates.

2. You Find the Money—or You Get Creative

Being all in means finding capital. Maybe it is from investors, maybe it's from selling your boat or taking out a second mortgage or maybe it's sweat equity and 20-hour days. But don't tell me you believe in your brand if you won't put your own skin in the game.

I have seen founders raise $100,000 with zero traction and I have seen bootstrapped brands break into Costco on grit alone. The variable isn't luck—it's commitment.

3. You Master Distribution, Not Just Instagram

CPG is not a popularity contest. It is a distribution game. Followers don't move cases. Velocity does. If you are more focused on follower count than on sell-through, you're chasing the wrong metric.

Being all in means understanding the brick-and-mortar play, the broker network, the distributor margin stack, the retail reset calendar and the slotting fee game. It means playing offense and defense with your marketing dollars.

You are not here to go viral. You are here to dominate shelf space and move product.

4. You Don't Ask for Permission

You don't wait for a Whole Foods buyer to discover you. You show up. You cold-call. You pitch until someone says "yes." Or until you have worn them down to the last "no."

The all-in founder is not polite. They are relentless. They don't care about gatekeepers because they know the goal is to get on the shelf, drive velocity and own the category—one store at a time if they must.

The Pain of Playing Halfway

I have worked with founders who had the next billion-dollar brand sitting in their hands, but they could not let go of their safety net. Do you know what happened? Nothing. The brand died quietly. It didn't fail dramatically; it just faded, like so many do.

And it was not because the product was bad. It was because the founder tried to coast.

They thought a good product was enough. It is not.

They thought a part-time effort would yield full-time success. It will not.

They thought being cautious was smart. In this game, caution is cowardice in disguise.

You either leap, or you lose.

Retail Doesn't Care About Your Feelings

Let me give it to you straight: Retail doesn't care about you.

They care about turns. They care about margin. They care about planograms, logistics and whether your product will move 12 units per store per week. They don't care that your grandma used the recipe. They don't care that you are passionate. They care that your product sells.

You want shelf space? You better come with data, dollars and a damn good reason to bump someone else off that shelf.

This is why being partially committed doesn't work. You don't have the luxury of being "kind of" serious about retail. It is a full-time battlefield, and it demands a full-time warrior.

You'll Bleed Before You Win

Let me be honest with you: This will be the hardest thing you've ever done.

You will lose money. You will lose friends. You will get knocked down. You will have inventory rot in a warehouse, ads that don't work and buyers who ghost you. You will want to quit.

That is the price of entry.

But if you are all in—really all in—you will get up every damn time. You'll pivot. You'll iterate. You'll find the angle. And eventually, you'll win. Not because it was easy, but because you refused to quit.

Why Being All In Is the Only Way Forward

We are entering the most competitive era in the history of CPG. The barriers to entry are low, but the barriers to scale are brutal. Retailers are shrinking shelf space. Supply chains are tighter. Consumers are more distracted than ever. The only brands that will survive are the ones that refuse to play halfway.

The winners are the ones who go in with conviction, capital, courage and clarity. The ones who don't ask, "What if I fail?" but instead declare, "I will win—or die trying."

This is not a test run. This is your legacy. If you are not willing to go all in, do something else. Seriously. Save yourself the pain. Because unless you are pregnant with purpose and fully committed, then you are already behind someone who is.

This Is Your Gut-Check Moment

This piece is not meant to scare you. It's meant to wake you up.

If you are sitting on a great product and waiting for the stars to align, stop. There is no perfect time. No perfect plan. Just the decision to commit—and go.

You're not launching a product. You're declaring war on the status quo. You're rewriting category rules. And if you're not willing to give it everything, don't be surprised when it gives you nothing.

Because like I said at the start—you cannot be partially pregnant. And you sure as hell can't build a CPG empire on part-time effort.

So...are you in?

Rule 27 Questions

- Are you all in and have you burned all the boats?
- Have you given up on plan B?
- Are you thinking about today but planning for next year?
- Have you planned cash needs for two years out?
- Are you willing to do whatever it takes, ethically, to achieve?

BONUS RULE 28

AI IS REAL AND IT'S NOT GOING AWAY

"Once a new technology rolls over you, if you're not part of the
steamroller, you're part of the road."
—Stewart Brand

The reason this is the bonus rule at the end of the list is simply because this rule applies to everything and looks into the future. This rule is simple: You must integrate AI (Artificial Intelligence) into almost every aspect of your brand and business.

The truth is that, as of this writing, we are all trying to figure out how AI will impact our businesses and lives. This technology is in its infancy and already having profound impacts.

Many people in the brick-and-mortar consumer-packaged goods business think AI is something for tech companies in Silicon Valley. If this is you, you're already behind. AI isn't a side project for coders—it's a freight train running straight through your planograms, your P+L and your customer relationships.

AI is not "coming someday." It's already here. Retailers, CPG manufacturers, distributors and even packaging suppliers are deploying AI quietly, and those who adopt fastest will define the playing field for the next 20 years.

A 2025 study conducted by Cisco shows that 97% of CEOs plan to integrate AI into their operations. However, the same study revealed that only 1.7% of these CEOs feel prepared to do so.

Ford Motor Company CEO Jim Farley recently warned that up to 50% of Ford white-collar workers will be eliminated by AI. Meanwhile, a 2025 Goldman Sachs research report projects AI could displace 6% to 7% of the entire US workforce.

This report outlines exactly how AI will touch every single aspect of the brick-and-mortar CPG ecosystem—from product development and supply chain to merchandising, pricing and shopper marketing—in plain language, without tech-industry fluff.

You may be wondering how AI can impact the CPG industry. Here are some of the initial thoughts on ways to harness and deploy AI:

1. Product Development: AI as Your R+D Superpower

The most expensive mistake in the CPG business is a failed product launch. Historically, we've relied on trend reports, focus groups and gut instinct to decide which new SKUs to create. AI turns that guessing game into a data-driven precision strike.

Trendspotting at Machine Speed: AI can scrape social media, search data, recipe sites and podcasts to spot emerging flavor trends or health concerns months before a human analyst would notice.

Formulation Optimization: AI-driven molecular analysis can suggest ingredient swaps that maintain taste and texture while reducing costs or improving nutrition.

2. Packaging: From Eye-Catching to Algorithm-Approved

Packaging is becoming a live feedback loop. AI can model consumer eye-tracking, dwell time and emotional response to a label before creating a physical sample, saving cost and time.

Personalization in Packaging: AI can drive hyper-localized packaging runs that align with neighborhood demographics—highlighting certain health claims or using language variants.

3. Supply Chain: Real-Time, Self-Healing Networks

AI replaces the old "forecast and hope" model with predictive demand planning, blending historical sales, weather data, local events and competitor promotions to forecast demand at the store-SKU level.

Self-Optimizing Logistics: AI can detect a potential supply disruption and automatically reroute shipments or reprioritize production runs without human intervention.

4. Retailer Relationships: Speaking the Same Data Language

Joint Business Planning Powered by AI: Both manufacturers and retailers can access AI-cleaned, real-time POS data, layered with loyalty behavior, basket composition and third-party insights.

Retail Media Integration: AI ensures your brand's retail media spend is targeted at customers most likely to convert in store.

5. In-Store Merchandising: Precision, Not Guesswork

Computer Vision for Shelf Compliance: AI-powered cameras can scan shelves in seconds, identify misplaced items and flag out-of-stocks.

Heat Mapping Shopper Movement: AI processes in-store traffic to optimize endcap placement, secondary displays and impulse-buy spots.

6. Pricing: Dynamic Without the Whiplash

Localized Competitive Pricing: Electronic shelf labels and AI can adjust prices based on local competition, inventory or promotions.

Elasticity Modeling: AI can predict how small price changes impact unit sales by store, week and product.

7. Marketing: Closing the Loop Between Digital and Physical

True Omnichannel Campaigns: AI links loyalty, mobile and in-store data to deliver personalized offers and measure their in-store effectiveness.

Creative Optimization: Generative AI creates ad variations tuned for micro-segments of your audience.

Even many of the online and TV commercials we will be using will be creatively directed by humans, but AI-generated.

8. Customer Experience: AI as the Silent Salesperson

Smart Kiosks and Mobile Assistance: AI-powered kiosks answer questions, suggest recipes and guide shoppers.

Personalized In-Aisle Messaging: AI can push relevant notifications as a shopper passes your product.

9. Sustainability and Compliance: Proving It, Not Just Saying It

AI can track supply-chain carbon footprint, verify sourcing and audit compliance with environmental or labeling regulations automatically.

10. The Competitive Divide: Why This Is a Now Problem

In every tech shift, there's a point where leaders pull so far ahead that laggards never catch up. In CPG brick-and-mortar, that point is approaching fast.

My Guidance for AI Use in Brick-and-Mortar CPG

1. **Start with one use case.**

Don't jump in and try to use AI for everything. Start with one thing and go deep in that area as opposed to just scratching the surface in too many directions.

2. **Invest in data quality.**

Data is important in most industries, but this is particularly true in an industry that is all about the numbers. As it comes to data and AI, are you paying for data or just trying to skim off the internet for free? Much of what you need is behind paywalls, so all the AI in the world isn't going to help you for deeper, specific data.

3. Train your people.

Your team needs to learn how to skillfully use AI. But they need to understand that if all they do is type something into AI and use that answer, that's not skillful, and it isn't harnessing the power of AI. There are plenty of people who know how to type, and Google can provide similar information.

Your team needs to learn how to use AI for deeper information and some insights. It's all about the prompts that are entered in. They need to ask the right questions or provide the correct directives to get more useful information. AI can help, but your team still has to employ critical thinking.

Your people also need to understand that they need to determine when AI is having a delusion. It can be difficult, but they must discern when AI is wrong, because sometimes it hallucinates. If AI can't find an answer on the internet, it tends to make one up.

4. Measure relentlessly.

The CPG world is a numbers game, so you should always be measuring. In the case of AI and usage, one of the things you should measure is how much employees are deploying and leveraging AI.

Finally, piggybacking on the previous point, measure what comes back from AI for accuracy.

5. Partner strategically.

View AI not as just a tool, but as a collaborator. AI can essentially be a member of the team. Your team can check with it, then take the response and go deeper or pivot directions, just as they might when collaborating with a coworker. But remember to fact check as needed.

6. **Protect the brand.**

As AI is developing, SEO is becoming less impactful. Google has seen a significant drop in searches because as AI takes a more prominent role, you can't buy the search terms to influence it or get around it. You will need a strategy for AI-optimization. This will likely include more verifiable, credible content from important sources. These are what AI looks for.

Closing: The AI Edge

AI adoption in CPG brick-and-mortar is not a trend—it is a structural change. Winners will integrate AI into every link of the value chain. The losers will still be debating as their competitors take their space.

Bonus Rule Questions

- Have you examined all the ways AI can impact and/or make your business better?
- Do you have an AI plan or strategy for your business?
- Are you treating AI as a tool or a collaborator?

SUMMARY

"Discipline is the bridge between goals and accomplishment."
—Jim Rohn

The Rules Work—If You Work Them

If you have made it this far in the book, you have obviously read all 27 rules. You now have the blueprint for success. Brands that have followed the rules have all been successful with many of them exiting their companies for hundreds of millions in cash.

You may not have noticed, but the rules follow a specific order. The reason for this is simple and is one of the reasons that the 27 rules always work. If you are brutally honest with yourself and you adhered to every rule, you will have pulled the plug already on a bad product that will not succeed. If you have gotten this far, are still pursuing this product and have been honest with yourself, you have met the following standards for your products (Rules 1-12):

- You have a product you are passionate about.

- It solves real problems or needs.
- It is not trying to be a Swiss army knife.
- It is not a "me too" item.
- It fits one or more of the three levers or pathways of retail.
- You can describe it in one sentence.
- Your product has mass appeal.
- You have legally identified that you can make the desired claims.
- You are marketing a premium product.
- You have secured at least a five to one margin.

If your product has cleared all these hurdles, you are now in position to execute on the balance of the 27 rules. But I want to warn you, these are not suggestions—this is not a situation where you can meet some of the rules and hope that luck or desire alone will make up for the missing ones.

Do not fall victim to the sunk-cost fallacy. There is no question that launching a product into retail is a monumental undertaking, and it will test your resolve on more than one occasion.

You will need the ability to keep pushing on in the face of adversity, but there is a difference between pushing through and pushing on. Think about the definition of sunk-cost fallacy from *Oxford Languages*:

"The phenomenon whereby a person is reluctant to abandon a strategy or course of action because they have invested heavily in it, even when it is clear that abandonment would be more beneficial."

Of course, a great deal of that investment is financial. But understand that the heavy investment is not just dollars. It includes your hopes, dreams and, as I indicated before, your ego. Remember Rule 22: *All Success Starts with the Truth*. At this point, there may be no more important rule. You must be a truth-seeker and truth-teller. If it is time to walk away, it will be painful. But what will the pain be 18 months further down the line if you don't walk away now?

Many businesses suffer with this issue, including some of the largest corporations in the world. It is difficult when you feel you are so invested into a bad idea that you cannot just walk away and take the loss. Here are some examples:

1. **Concorde** (British and French Governments)

What happened:
The Concorde supersonic jet program, a joint venture between the British and French governments (British Aircraft Corporation and Aérospatiale), was massively over budget and behind schedule. Despite knowing the plane would likely never be commercially viable due to its high operational costs and limited passenger capacity, both governments kept funding it because they had already invested billions.

Result:

- According to BAE Systems, the estimated cost was over $1.6 billion (in 1970s dollars)
- Only 20 Concordes were ever built
- Program was shut down in 2003 after years of losses
- The term "Concorde Fallacy" became synonymous with sunk-cost fallacy

2. **Quibi** (Short-form streaming platform)

What happened:
Founded by Jeffrey Katzenberg and led by CEO Meg Whitman, Quibi launched in April 2020 with over $1.75 billion in investor backing. Despite early signs that users did not want short-form content on a subscription app, the company doubled down on spending, marketing and content creation.

Result:

- Lost nearly $1.4 billion
- Refused to pivot or slow spending despite lack of traction
- Shut down after just six months
- Example of sticking with a flawed business model to justify initial investment

3. **Microsoft** (Nokia acquisition)

What happened:
In 2013, Microsoft acquired Nokia's mobile phone division for $7.2 billion, hoping to gain a competitive edge in smartphones. After the acquisition, the Windows Phone still failed to gain market share against Android and Apple's iOS. Microsoft kept pouring money into the platform, trying to salvage the investment rather than cutting losses early.

Result:

- Microsoft eventually wrote off $7.6 billion in losses
- Laid off over 18,000 employees
- Ended all mobile phone development by 2017
- Sunk-cost fallacy led to prolonged support for a doomed product

Each of these cases shows how decision-makers allowed past investment to override logic and data, leading to larger losses than if they had cut bait earlier. The sunk-cost fallacy is especially dangerous in corporate strategy because it disguises itself as "commitment" or "long-term thinking."

This is the same behavior that compels a chronic gambler to keep doubling down when they are losing money. It is the feeling that *I am in so deep I cannot stop now*. Notice that it is the "feeling"—not logic—which is leading in the sunk-cost fallacy.

This is the reason we asked so many tough questions in the beginning of the 27 rules—you must be honest enough with yourself to "kill all your darlings" if they do not pass the test. All the effort and great marketing in the world cannot make a bad product successful for very long. Even Microsoft, with its virtually unlimited resources, could not keep a bad product alive.

Let me give it to you straight: The rules only work if you follow them. That sounds simple, even obvious, but in business, especially in the cutthroat world of CPG, I see people break this principle every day and then wonder why they are bleeding cash or losing shelf space.

Here's another hard truth: The universe, like the market, rewards discipline. It punishes chaos. The rules for success in the CPG business are not some abstract philosophy or suggestions on a corporate retreat flip chart. They are more like gravity. Sure, you can choose to ignore them, but don't act surprised when you hit the pavement.

In this business, we know what the rules are. You are literally holding them in your hands. An abridged summary:

- Understand your consumer better than they understand themselves.
- Build products that solve problems.
- Price it right.
- Support it with real advertising—not just "impressions," but actual influence.
- And for God's sake, don't get cute with retail. Retailers do not care how special your story is if your product doesn't turn.

But what do so many founders do? They skip steps. They

shortcut the process. They "feel" their way through it like they are Steve Jobs in a vision quest, forgetting he actually followed the rules of product-market fit, supply-chain discipline and world-class marketing better than anyone.

I have built dozens of brands. My team and I have helped founders go from garage to national players. And I have had my teeth kicked in on the way. You do not get a Guinness World Record, grow companies or stay in the fight for 30-plus years without getting religious about the rules.

Now let me be clear—I am not talking about bureaucracy or asking permission. I am not telling you to color inside the lines for the sake of coloring inside the lines. I am telling you that the fundamentals exist for a reason. Learn them. Master them. Then, if you want to innovate, you will do it from a solid position of knowledge, not ignorance.

You do not get to scale a brand by throwing spaghetti at the wall and hoping a TikTok goes viral. You get there by knowing the rules that govern your category, as well as your channel and your customers. With that knowledge, you can then execute them with military precision.

As I mentioned, I am a race car driver. In racing, there are rules too. You don't just step into a car and gun it. You respect the machine. You learn the track. You follow the protocols that keep you alive and moving fast. Break the rules, and at best, you lose. At worst, you crash. Business is no different.

So if you are building something, especially in the CPG world, ask yourself: Am I following the real rules? Not the ones I made up. Not the ones my buddy with a Shopify store told me. The real, time-tested rules of product, marketing, distribution and velocity.

Because, I repeat: The rules work. But only if you follow them.

How to Lead Your Team and Scale with Purpose

*"You don't build a business, you build people—and then people build
the business."*
—Zig Ziglar

If you are leading a team in the consumer-packaged goods
space and you do not have a crystal-clear sense of purpose, you
are already losing. And if you are scaling without purpose,
you're just accelerating your way into chaos. In this business,
scaling without purpose is like putting a jet engine on a lawn
chair; it might move fast, but it is going nowhere good.

The truth is, scaling a business is not just about adding
more zeros to your revenue. It is about alignment. It is about
building something that compounds—not collapses—under
pressure. I have coached, built, advertised for and sometimes
salvaged CPG brands at every stage of the journey. And here is
what I know: Your growth is only as strong as your leadership
and your leadership is only as strong as the clarity of
your purpose.

The Purpose-Driven Leader

Purpose is not some squishy, HR-brochure buzzword. It is the
operational north star of your organization. It tells your team
why they show up, *how* to make decisions and *what* to fight for
when the winds shift. And believe me, the wind always shifts.

When your team knows what the business stands for, you
eliminate 90% of hesitation and confusion. You create a decision-making framework. You reduce friction. People self-
correct because the mission guides them. But here's the kicker:
They won't follow your mission unless *you* live it out loud. You
—the founder, the CEO, the brand builder—need to embody

the purpose. Not in meetings, but in how you hire, fire, market and serve your customers. Your actions provide the definition of what you—your business—stand for.

You want to build a team of patriots, not mercenaries. Patriots fight for a cause, while mercenaries fight for the money. You must demonstrate the cause clearly so they can decide their motivation.

Build Leaders, Not Just Employees

Scaling with purpose demands that you stop thinking of your team as employees and start thinking of them as future leaders. Why? Because at scale, you can't make every decision yourself. And if you try, your business becomes a bottleneck. Leadership isn't about control—it's about multiplication. Your job is to create leaders who can create more leaders.

This means investing in the kind of training that is not just about tasks, but about mindset. Teaching people how to think, not just what to do. That's what separates the CPG brands that hit $5 million and stall from the ones that break through $50 million and keep climbing.

Operationalize the Vision

Purpose is nice on a mission statement, but unless it shows up in your systems, it's just marketing. You need to operationalize your purpose. That means building your supply chain, your product development cycle, your advertising strategy and your retail partnerships around your values and goals.

Are you a clean-label brand? Then every vendor, every ingredient and every ad campaign better reflect that. Are you about democratizing wellness? Then your pricing, your packaging and your distribution plan better match that story. Alignment between what you say and how you operate builds trust.

And trust is the only brand equity that scales faster than media dollars.

Remove the Middle Layer of Mediocrity

When companies scale, they start to layer up. More managers. More meetings. More "alignment calls" that burn an hour and produce nothing but consensus at the speed of molasses. My advice? Cut the fat. Middle management often becomes middle *muddling*. Protect the velocity of your business by keeping your structure flat, communication sharp and decision-making fast.

This is especially true in CPG where speed-to-shelf matters. The longer your team takes to decide on packaging, formulations or ad creative, the more likely it is that someone else beats you to it. Scale should amplify speed, not kill it.

Culture Is Not Perks—It Is Performance

People talk a lot about culture when scaling. They think it's about adding cold brew on tap and unlimited PTO. That is not culture. Culture is what people do when you are not in the room. It is the standards they hold each other to. It is how they deal with a lost retail slot, a bad shipment or a product recall.

In a purpose-driven scale-up, culture has to be weaponized for performance. That does not mean burnout. It means clarity. It means ownership. It means outcomes over optics. If someone is not performing, it's not personal; it's mission critical. Every person in the organization should know that scale depends on execution, not excuses.

Metrics With Meaning

If you do not measure it, you cannot manage it. But in scale, most companies start measuring the wrong things. Vanity metrics like impressions, followers or "brand sentiment" start creeping in. Forget that. You want meaningful metrics like:

- Customer acquisition cost
- LTV (Lifetime Value)
- Gross margin
- Retail velocity
- Trade spend efficiency
- Inventory turns

These are real numbers that tie back to real health.

Scale demands discipline in measurement. It's not just about growth. It's about profitable growth. And if you cannot see it, you cannot steer it. Your dashboard should be the heartbeat of your business, and everyone on your team should understand what those numbers mean.

Adapt Relentlessly, But Don't Drift

Here's a paradox: The faster you scale, the more you have to adapt, and the more tempted you are to drift from your purpose. Don't drift. Stay focused. Adaptation is tactical; purpose is strategic. Don't confuse the two.

Change how you execute. Change your go-to-market. Change your price if you must. But never change who you are. Once your brand starts shifting to chase short-term wins, it stops being a brand and becomes a commodity. Commodities compete on price. Brands compete on meaning.

Own the Hard Stuff

Let's be real: Scaling with purpose is hard. It means saying "no" to easy money. It means walking away from deals that do not fit your values. It means having tough conversations with people you once considered irreplaceable. But leadership is not about being liked; it is about being respected. If your team knows you'll make the hard calls to protect the mission, they'll follow you through a brick wall.

In the CPG space, the brands that scale and last—the ones that become household names—are led by founders who aren't just chasing revenue. They are chasing impact. They know why they are here, and they build teams, systems and cultures that reflect that purpose.

So if you are leading a team, ask yourself: Are we scaling on purpose? Or are we just getting bigger? Because in this business, bigger is not always better. But better always results in bigger.

WHERE TO GO FROM HERE

"The first step towards getting somewhere is to decide that you're not going to stay where you are."
—J.P. Morgan

First, if you are here, it means you dedicated some significant time out of your life to reading these words. I want to personally thank you for giving me this time and for sticking with the content of the book. It is a humbling experience to know that people have given me their attention, and I do not take your time lightly. Time is the one resource that you cannot bank, borrow or get back.

Let's assume you have followed all 27 rules and you a) haven't stopped making the product because it's not viable and b) have honestly decided that you can successfully move forward. Congratulations! Now it is time to assemble your resources, build your team and expand your knowledge. Investing in your own education is never a bad bet; learning should be a lifetime endeavor and is a key to success, while not learning is usually a recipe for disaster.

Other Books

Let's start with other books you should read. My number one recommendation is *The Science of Scaling*, from my good friend Dr. Benjamin Hardy. Ben is a brilliant thinker and has written a road map for how to rapidly grow your business in a very short time frame.

Ben has co-written several books with another great friend of mine, Dan Sullivan. Dan is the co-founder of Strategic Coach®, the number one business coaching operation on the planet. He is also a brilliant deep thinker. There are three books in this series: *10x is Easier Than 2x*®, *The Gap and The Gain*® and *Who Not How*®. If you want to join the top coaching group in the world, you will find it at strategiccoach.com.

Next comes yet another good friend, Joe Polish, the most connected man on the planet. He has years of hard-won wisdom to share with you. His latest book is *What's In It For Them?* Joe also runs the number one mastermind group in the world, where you can learn deep insights into marketing, become a better entrepreneur and connect with nearly anyone in the world. You will find it at geniusnetwork.com.

Gino Wickman is an entrepreneur who helps entrepreneurs work more impactfully in their businesses and lives. His books include *Rocket Fuel, Entrepreneurial Leap, Traction, The EOS Life* and *Shine: How Looking Inward Is the Key to Unlocking True Entrepreneurial Freedom*. In *Shine*, he covers his 10 Disciplines framework that can help maximize your energy and impact.

As mentioned earlier, Dr. Doug Brackmann's book *Driven* is a fascinating look at the entrepreneurial brain. Doug shares information on the genetic gift that manifests into tremendous drive and how you can harness it for success.

All four (five when you count Dan Sullivan) of the above authors also do podcasts, which I highly recommend.

Staying with podcasts, the best podcast on the topic of the

CPG industry is called CPG Insiders, hosted by Justin Girouard and myself. Every episode is built around the daily conversations that we have with CPG clients and includes some of the best minds in the industry as guests. You can find it at cpginsiders.com.

Organizations

There are organizations that make sense for you to know about and maybe even join. The first is ECRM or Range Me. You can find them at ecrm.marketgate.com and rangeme.com. This is an especially important group to get to know. They run a platform for buyers and sellers to communicate and find each other, as well as monthly category-specific selling events.

If your product sells to mass drug retailers you need to look at NACDS (National Association of Chain Drug Stores). The membership is made up of every multi-outlet pharmacy in the country, and they run a major national event called TSE (Total Store Expo) which brings large numbers of retailers and suppliers together. You can find more information at nacds.org and tse.nacds.org.

If you are in the specialty food world, you would want to look at the Specialty Food Association and the Fancy Food Shows they produce. You can find them at specialtyfood.com.

If you live in the organic or health food world, you cannot miss the shows known as Expo West and the smaller version once named Expo East but now called Newtopia Now. Their sites are expowest.com and newtopianow.com.

Now, what is the number one resource for nearly everything else you need? This would include advertising, marketing, package design, go-to-market branding and strategy and introductions to the best brokers, experts, attorneys and leaders in the CPG world.

The answer is Jekyll+Hyde Labs (jekyllhydelabs.com or

JandHLabs.com). This is my firm of over 30 years, where we have launched and built hundreds of brands, thousands of SKUs, driven billions in sales and assisted our clients with company buyouts measured in billions.

We created the 27 Rules directly from these 30-plus years of experience. Over those years, we have had the ability to work hand in hand with the brands that have made it big and watched what happened to the brands that did not. Like this book, we are the cheat code to winning in CPG retail.

But be forewarned, we adhere to the 27 Rules and will continuously point you back to them when you try to take a short cut. We are the place to go when you want to grow your brand exponentially, not incrementally.

If at any time in your CPG journey you think I or my team can help you, please feel free to reach out to us at our website, JandHLabs.com. From there you can email or call us, or you can ask Virtual Mark, my AI clone (an example of how AI changes things), any question you have 24 hours per day.

ACKNOWLEDGEMENTS

There are not enough pages in this book to truly thank all of the people who, at some time over my life, poured into me wisdom, knowledge and spiritual leadership. This section is only a small reflection of the gratitude I feel.

First and always, to my wife and lifetime partner Summer —everything we do is an accomplishment by us both. Behind every so-called great man there is a much greater woman, and you have been that for me.

To my daughters Andi and Melissa, your love, patience and belief have carried me further than I could have walked alone. You gave me the gift of being a "Girl Dad." You've also given me the grounding that made it possible to keep chasing bigger visions. You have this magical way of bringing me back to earth whenever you feel it is necessary.

To my son, Mark Young 2—Mark^2: you are my force multiplier. My thinking, my wisdom, my sense of adventure and my strange sense of humor live on in you. You push me into new frontiers of AI and inspire me to rise higher, think sharper and build bigger. This work carries your imprint as much as mine.

To my late father Jack—your bizarre wisdom is only now coming into focus.

To my late, great friend and brother Chuck Woolery—you were the wisest and most naïve man alive, all at the same time. You left your mark on millions, but for those of us closest to you, you left a void that no one else will ever fill. Thank you for your friendship, your humor and your perspective, which I will carry for a lifetime.

To the Dead Hooker Society—Al, Steve, Doug, Luigi, Brandon, Tyler and the rest—you know what this means.

To Michelle Pike, whose sharp eye and tireless editing have kept these pages clear and true, and to Justin Girouard, who helped fill in the missing gaps with insight and precision.

To the entire Jekyll + Hyde team, who quietly bring new brands to life and cash the virtual checks that my mouth so often writes—thank you for turning bold promises into reality.

To David Biernbaum—thank you for opening the doors to insider knowledge and keeping me connected to the pulse of the industry.

To our friends in the trenches—the brokers, lawyers, scientists, accountants and colleagues who fight alongside us in the details—you are the unsung backbone of every CPG victory.

To the thinkers and mentors who sharpened my perspective: Dan Sullivan, Joe Polish, Dr. Ben Hardy, Gino Wickman, Dan Hibma, Mel Partovich and so many, many more—your wisdom has changed the way I lead, think and grow.

To the many mentors and guides who appeared at just the right time over the course of my life—you have inspired me and compelled me to pour into the lives of others. Your wisdom, delivered in the exact moments I needed it most, is carried forward here.

And to the thousands of people who have listened to my podcasts, read my books and papers, watched my videos or attended my talks—I am humbled that you chose to spend your valuable time with me.

Finally, to every client who trusted us over the past 30 years—thank you for giving us the runway to learn what works, what doesn't and how to turn consumer-packaged products into enduring successes. Without your courage and faith, there would have been no rulebook to write.

This book is a reflection of all of you—the mentors, the doers, the allies and the believers. Thank you for making this journey possible.

ABOUT THE AUTHOR

Dr. Mark Young is the CEO and founder of Jekyll+Hyde Labs, one of the nation's leading advertising agencies for consumer-packaged goods. He is in his fourth decade of being a brand accelerator for over 200 consumer-packaged goods. He has been responsible for billions in consumer sales and helping to engineer company exits now measured in the billions.

Mark had his first job in the advertising industry by the age of 12 and launched his first successful product into mass retail by the age of 13. He has previously authored *HYPNO-TI$ING: The Secrets & Science of Ads That Sell More* and is the host of the podcast CPG Insiders (cpginsiders.com).

Mark lives in Michigan and Florida with his wife Summer.

For more information about Mark Young and *The 27 Unbreakable Rules*, scan the QR code below:

ABOUT THE PUBLISHER

Legacy Launch Pad is a boutique publishing company that works with entrepreneurs from all over the world.

For more information about Legacy Launch Pad Publishing, go to: www.legacylaunchpadpub.com.